Christmas
make it
sparkle

225 Simple Crafts, Food & Decorating
Ideas For Your **Holiday Home**

CAROL FIELD DAHLSTROM

Brave Ink Press, Ankeny, Iowa

AUTHOR AND EDITOR
Carol Field Dahlstrom

BOOK DESIGN
Angie Haupert Hoogensen

PHOTOGRAPHY
Pete Krumhardt and Andy Lyons Cameraworks

WATERCOLOR ILLUSTRATIONS
Alice Wetzel

Copyediting: Susan Banker, Janet Figg
Proofreading: Jill Philby, Jan Temeyer
Recipe Development: Jennifer Petersen,
Ardith Field, Barbara Hoover
Recipe Testing: Elizabeth Dahlstrom,
Ardith Field
Technical Assistant: Judy Bailey
Photostyling: Carol Dahlstrom
Photostyling Assistant: Donna Chesnut
Technical Artwork: Shawn Drafahl
Location and Props: Roger Dahlstrom
Cover Photography: Pete Krumhardt
Separation: Quantum Imaging

*Thanks to those who have helped execute some
of the designs or recipes in this book: Susan Banker,
Donna Chesnut, Elizabeth Dahlstrom,
Michael Dahlstrom, Roger Dahlstrom, Ardith Field,
Barbara Hoover, Jennifer Petersen, Ann Smith,
Jan Temeyer, and Alice Wetzel*

ISBN 0-9679764-2-1
Library of Congress Control Number 2003092249

Printed in United States of America First Edition
Carol Field Dahlstrom, Inc. and Brave Ink Press strive to provide
high quality products and information that will make your life
happier and more beautiful. Please contact us with your comments,
questions, and suggestions or to inquire about purchasing books at
www.braveink.com or *e-mail* braveink@aol.com or write to:
Brave Ink Press, P.O. Box 663, Ankeny, Iowa 50021.

*Author and editor Carol Field Dahlstrom
has written, edited, and produced numerous
crafts, decorating, and holiday books, as
well as children's specialty products, for
17 years. She has shared her love of creating
and crafting with audiences throughout the
country through speaking engagements and
television appearances. Her products inspire
families to spend time together—creating, learning, and celebrating.
She lives in the country with her husband and children where
she writes and designs from her studio.*

Christmas is the most beautiful time of year. Colored lights *shimmer* in neighborhood windows, fresh evergreens are adorned with *glittering* ornaments, and snow *glistens* on the coated shoulders of carolers at the door. But it isn't just the windows and the trees and the warm woolen coats that *sparkle* with the coming of Christmas. You can see it in little eyes that *twinkle* when secrets are all around, and in the smiles of Mothers and Dads as they wrap the perfect gifts. You can hear the *brilliant* voices sharing Christmas music and you can feel the *glow* of families as they gather together for the holidays.

Your holiday home becomes the focal point for all of this marvelous activity and you want to share your talents with the ones you love. In this book you'll find ideas for beautiful ornaments and tree decorations, glorious wreaths and centerpieces, memorable handmade greeting cards, delicious recipes, stunningly simple decorations, clever gifts for everyone on your holiday list, and unique lighting ideas. All of these easy-to-make projects, recipes, and ideas will help make your holiday just a little *brighter*.

So as you *reflect* upon this most beautiful time of year, take time to feel the warmth of the season in your home, and in your heart, as you make this Christmas one that *sparkles*.

> "*I will honor Christmas in my heart and try to keep it all the year.*"
>
> —A Christmas Carol (1843)

Carol Field Dahlstrom

Contents

create some
shimmering
holiday goodies
from your kitchen
pages 76-123

make the season *bright*
with **festive**
decorating ideas
pages 124-153

put a *twinkle*
in their eyes with
gifts and **wraps** you make
pages 154-171

watch the
season *glow*
with **christmas lighting**
pages 172-185

About This Book

In this book you'll find projects, gifts, decorations, and recipes to make your holiday sparkle with the wonder of Christmas. You'll find simple projects that you can make during that exciting, but often too-busy, time of the year. To make your holiday go as smoothly as possible, we've added some quick-to-find symbols that should help you find the information you need even more quickly.

MAKING THE PROJECTS

Look for this symbol for a list of materials you need to make the project or recipe. We have given you general materials and sometimes we list what brand of product we used to make the project shown. Oftentimes we tell you where you might purchase the item. If the item is unusual we have given you a list of sources on page 191 that will give you an address or e-mail so you can order the item if you wish.

Look for this symbol when you are looking for the instructions on how to make the projects. Sometimes we have added step-by-step how-to photos to show you how to make the project more easily. Oftentimes we've included a picture of all of the items required to make the project.

We have included this visual picture of the materials required to show you just how simple the project is to make, even though the finished piece might look so exquisite it is hard to believe that it was made with such simple supplies.

THE PATTERNS

Most of the patterns in the book are full-size.

TREE
PATTERN

If the patterns were too large to fit on the page we have given you the pattern on a grid. We have also included a percentage that you can use to enlarge the pattern on a copy machine.

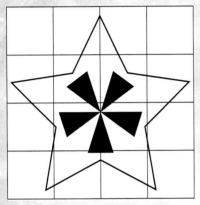

CUT OUT STAR   1 SQUARE = 1 INCH OR ENLARGE AT 200%

SAFETY FIRST

When you are making the projects, always remember safety first. When painting, always use adequate ventilation and follow the manufacturer's instructions on the bottle or can. Always use extreme care when using crafts knives or cutters of any type, and follow the manufacturer's instructions when using specialty materials.

AN ADDED BONUS

When you are creating the projects and recipes, we offer you even more ways to make your holiday more fulfilling.

 Look for this symbol to find some clever ways to make the project into a gift. When you see this symbol you'll find a quick gift wrap or other presentation idea.

 Look for this symbol for ways to work on a project or recipe together. Whether with family or friends, it is always more fun to craft or cook together.

 Look for this symbol if you want a very quick project. These projects are so easy to make they can usually be made in a matter of minutes.

THE RECIPES

The recipes in this book are family favorites from homes all over the country. They have been tested in kitchens just like yours and enjoyed by families at holiday time. All of the recipes can be made from ingredients that are easy to find and available in most parts of the country. Oftentimes we give you an idea for how to make the recipe into a wonderful food gift. Look for these food gift ideas throughout the chapter.

MORE IDEAS

At the end of each chapter you'll find even more ideas that you can use to make your holiday memorable.

CLIP ART

The lovely pictures on pages 186-189 can be used to make some of the projects in the book. Take the book to your local copy shop and ask for a color copy on cardstock.

The questionnaire on page 189 can be mailed in or answered online at www.braveink.com. We would love to hear from you. Merry Christmas!

"O Christmas Tree, how lovely
are thy branches!"
—Traditional Christmas Carol

see the
treetops
glisten
with
holiday
ornaments
and
garlands

9

Glittering Seashells

You may not be near the beach, but these from-the-ocean beauties are sure to bring a smile. Glistening like the sand itself, these shell trims can be colored to fit your holiday decor.

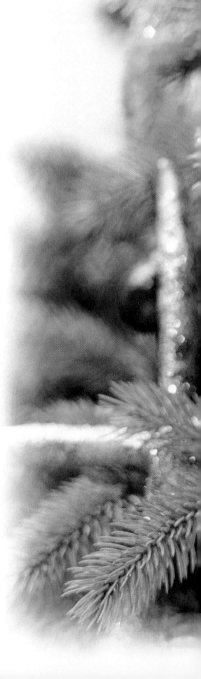

WHAT YOU NEED

Starfish and other small shells
(available at shell shops or
craft stores)
Drill and ⅛-inch drill bit
Crafts paint in desired colors
Paintbrush
Toothpick
Waxed paper
Tacky crafts glue
Fine glitter in color to
match paint
Fine monofilament thread

WHAT YOU DO

For the starfish, drill a hole at the top of the starfish and paint desired color. Place on waxed paper; cover with a layer of glue. Sprinkle with glitter. Reopen the hole with a toothpick. Thread the monofilament through the hole to hang. *For the shell garland,* drill a hole near the top of each shell and paint desired colors. Place on waxed paper; cover shell front with glue. Sprinkle with glitter. Use the toothpick to reopen the hole. Tie a knot at thread end. Thread shells onto line, knotting before and after each shell. Tie a knot at the end of the thread.

Whether you use antique or new glass crystals, these elegant baubles are sure to add sparkle and beauty to your tree.

Holiday Crystals

MAKE IT A GIFT

PAINT THE CRYSTALS USING COLORS TO MATCH THE COLOR SCHEME OF THE HOME OF THE LUCKY PERSON RECEIVING THE GIFT. PAINT THE WRAPPING USING THE SAME PATTERNS AS THE ORNAMENTS.

WHAT YOU NEED

Plain white paper
Purchased glass crystals (lamp
  decorations); glass paints
Finely pointed small paintbrushes
24-gauge colored wire

WHAT YOU DO

Referring to the patterns, *below*, and the photo, *above*, practice painting the design on paper. Tiny, simple designs work best. Choose crystals with many flat areas. *For the tree,* paint the green shape first and let dry. Add the dots and star. *For the garland,* paint color dots of one color first, leaving space between the dots; let dry. Add the other color dots painting all the dots of each color at one time. Bake the crystals following manufacturer's instructions. Allow to cool. Thread a piece of wire through the hole at the top; twist together to form hanger.

HOLIDAY CRYSTAL PATTERNS

Beaded Beauties

Delicate mini-beads glitter in the light to form the designs on these simple yet elegant trims. Match the glitter and beads to the color of the ornament to make a beautifully-subtle statement.

WHAT YOU NEED

*Purchased matte-finish
  ornaments in desired colors*

Small tumbler

*Large flat-bottom bowl or
  baking pan*

*Clear crafts glue (such
  as Suze Gluez)*

Micro beads

*Fine glitter to
  match beads*

MAKE IT TONIGHT

These beaded beauties can be made in about an hour. Work on three or four ornaments at a time and you'll have a complete set in an evening.

WHAT YOU DO

Place the ornament in the tumbler and place in the pan. This will allow you to work on one side at a time and catch the tiny beads so they can be reused. Referring to the pattern, *below*, use the glue to draw the outline of the leaf and vine design on one side of the ornament. Sprinkle the glitter on the design. Fill the inside of the leaves with glue. Sprinkle with the micro beads. Allow to dry and repeat for the other side.

LEAF AND VINE
PATTERN

Taking their cue from shimmering
Christmas snow, these lovely
ornaments are covered in white
wax and glitter. No two are
ever alike.

Snow-touched Ornaments

✦ WHAT YOU NEED

*Purchased matte-finish
  ornament; white candle wax
Small can, saucepan, and heat
  source for melting wax
Custard cup or small dish
Old spoon; fine white glitter*

✦ WHAT YOU DO

Break up the wax and place in the small can. Place the can in the saucepan half filled with water (see photo 1). Melt the wax in the saucepan filled with water on the stove or hot plate just until it is melted. *Do not overheat and never place the wax in the microwave.* Place the ornament in the custard cup. Use the spoon to pour the wax over the ornament (see photo 2). It will set immediately. Carefully rotate the ornament and keep adding wax until the desired look is achieved. Dust with fine white glitter before the wax is completely dry.

What could be
more beautiful
than fresh
flowers on your
evergreen?
These tiny vials
catch the light
and hold water
to keep the
flowers fresh
for days.

Petite Rose Vases

 WHAT YOU NEED

Tiny glass vials
  (available at crafts stores)
Fine red wire (24-gauge)
Wire cutters
Small shank-style buttons
Fresh small-bloom roses

MAKE IT TOGETHER

LET THE CHILDREN HELP CHOOSE THE HOLIDAY BUTTONS
TO DECORATE THESE CLEVER TRIMS. KIDS WILL ALSO LOVE PUTTING
THE FRESH FLOWER IN THE TINY VIAL AS IT ADORNS THE TREE.

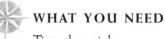 **WHAT YOU DO**

Remove the cork from the vial. Cut an 8-inch length of wire and loop the end. Position the wire at the base of the vial; wind the wire around the vial and make a hook at the top. Cut off the excess wire. Slide the wire off the vial and string buttons on the wire. Put the wire and buttons back on the vial with the hook at the top. Add water and a fresh rose and hang on the tree.

Faux Ribbon Candy

The bright colors of holiday ribbon candy bring smiles to all who see them. Make this polymer clay version of the popular candy to hang on your tree.

WHAT YOU NEED

Polymer clay in desired colors
(such as Sculpey)
Knife; rolling pin
Waxed paper; toothpick
Crafts glue; white glitter; thread

WHAT YOU DO

Cut three slices of clay each about ¼-inch thick and about 1×1 inch in diameter. Stack the pieces together. Turn the clay on its side and using a rolling pin, roll out the clay on the waxed paper until it is approximately 1×5 inches long stretching the clay to reach the length but keeping the layers as even as possible. Use the knife to even off the sides and ends so the layered piece is about ¾×4 inches when trimmed. Fold the layered clay back and forth in ribbon-candy style. Poke a hole in the top with the toothpick. Bake the clay following manufacturer's instructions. Cool. Coat the edges of the clay with crafts glue and sprinkle with glitter. Let dry. Put the thread in the hole and tie a knot for a hanger.

Let the light shine through these crisp
vellum trims. So easy to make, you can
fill your tree in no time with glorious gift
envelopes and pretty poinsettias.

Pretty Vellum Trims

WHAT YOU NEED

(For each Vellum Envelope)

Tracing paper; pencil; scissors
8½×11-inch sheet of colored
  vellum (available at crafts stores)

Decorative scissors
Paper punch
18-inch length of ½-inch
  ribbon to match vellum color

WHAT YOU DO

Enlarge envelope pattern
on *page 20* onto tracing
paper. Cut out. Trace
around the pattern onto
the vellum, marking folds
and dots. Cut out the
vellum using decorative
scissors. Fold pattern as
indicated on the dotted
fold lines, folding bottom
flap first, then side flaps.
Match up hole marks and
punch. Thread ribbon
through the holes. Tie a
knot or bow in the front.
Fill with gold shredded
paper and the desired gift.

continued on page 20

Pretty Vellum Trims continued

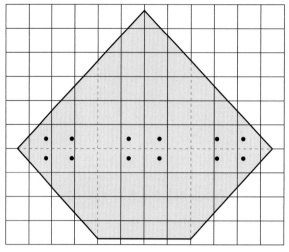

ENVELOPE PATTERN

1 SQUARE = 1 INCH
OR ENLARGE AT 400%

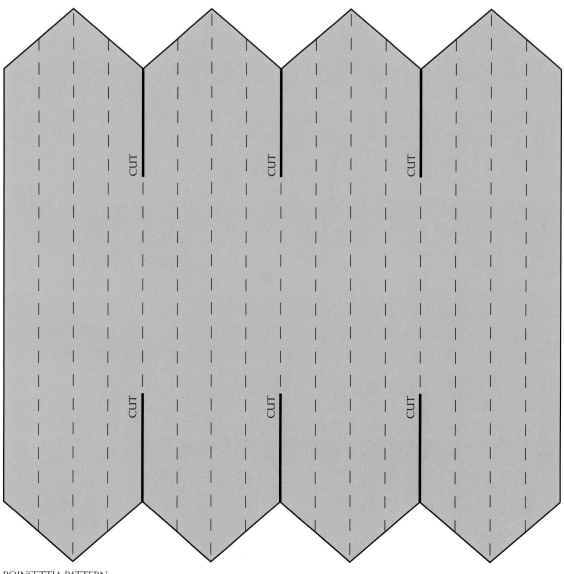

CUT

CUT

CUT

CUT

CUT

CUT

POINSETTIA PATTERN

String the beads onto the chenille stem. Push them to the middle of the chenille stem. Set aside. Trace and cut out the full size pattern, *page 20,* onto tracing paper. Trace around it on the vellum and cut out. Mark the fold and cut lines. Fold the poinsettia back and forth on the dashed lines like an accordion. Pinch at the middle and secure in place with the chenille stem and beads. Push the beads to the front of the flower. Twist the chenille stems to the back to secure. Gently pull the petals apart. The vellum is crisp and will keep its shape after opening up the folds. Adjust the beads as needed. Use the chenille stem ends on the back to secure the poinsettia on the tree.

WHAT YOU NEED

(For each Poinsettia Trim)

Tracing paper; pencil
Eight to ten gold beads or beads
* in desired colors*
Gold chenille stem
Scissors

One 8½×11-inch sheet of colored vellum or printed scrapbook paper (available at scrapbook or craft stores)

These charming ornaments were designed to emulate the look of the 1950s version of the metallic birds. See the real cousin of these fun-loving birds, right.

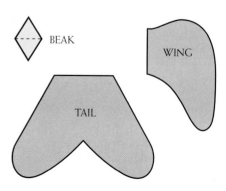

Friendly Bird Trims

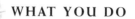

WHAT YOU NEED
(for one bird)

One 1½-inch diameter foam
   ball and one 1-inch diameter
   foam ball (such as Styrofoam)
Toothpicks
Small scrap of cardstock in the
   color to match the bird
Couscous pasta
Decoupage medium; paintbrush
Small dish
Round plastic foam disc
Metallic spray paint in
   desired color
White glitter; two googly eyes
Gold metallic chenille stem
½ inch wooden spool
1-inch flat wooden disc
Black paint; black glitter
Strong crafts glue (such as
   E6000)
Short straight pin
Fine monofilament for hanging

WHAT YOU DO

Break the toothpick in half. Attach the two foam balls using the toothpick (see photo 1). Cut the tail, beak, and wings from cardstock using the patterns, *below*. Cut slits in the foam body for the cardstock pieces. Push the pieces into the foam ball. Add a dot of crafts glue at the slits to secure. Use a toothpick to position the bird in the foam disc as a base as you work (see photo 2). In the disposable dish, mix the couscous and enough decoupage medium to coat the pasta. Working on one side at a time, paint the couscous mixture on the bird. Allow to dry.

BEAK

WING

TAIL

Turn the bird over and use the couscous/decoupage mixture on the other side (see photo 3). Cover the entire bird with the mixture. Allow to dry. Leave the bird on the foam base and spray-paint with desired color. Dust immediately with fine white glitter. Allow to dry. Glue eyes to bird head. Make hat by gluing the spool to the wood disc. Paint the hat black and dust with black glitter. Allow to dry. Glue to the top of the bird head using a strong crafts glue. Cut the chenille stem in half; wrap around the bird neck. Cut a 6-inch length of monofilament, loop it, and pin to center of the bird for hanging.

Fill an antique bowl with these jewel-toned pieces for a lovely centerpiece. Make a set in colors to match your holiday decor.

Royal Baubles

WHAT YOU NEED

Purchased matte-finish
  ornaments
Small tumbler
Clear crafts glue (such as
  Suze Gluez)
Fine gold glitter
Gold permanent marking pen

WHAT YOU DO

Place an ornament in the tumbler. Start at the top and make curly lines, zigzags, or swirls radiating from the top using the marking pen. Turn the ornament on its side and work on one side at a time. Place dots of glue in a row about a third of the way down the ornament or straight down from the top. Dust with glitter. Let dry. Continue adding swirls or zigzags with marking pen and dots with glitter until the desired look is achieved. Allow ornament to dry.

MAKE IT TONIGHT

GOLDEN GLITTER AND A GOLD MARKING PEN ARE ALL IT TAKES TO MAKE THIS SET OF ORNAMENTS IN AN EVENING.

Golden Days Photos

Display your cherished photos on the tree in tiny golden frames. A touch of colored pencil on the vintage photos brings them to life.

WHAT YOU NEED

Small picture frames with holes or spaces in the frame

Gold spray paint

Black and white copies of favorite photos; colored pencils

Gold beads; fine gold wire

MAKE IT TOGETHER

MAKE EXTRA COPIES OF FAMILY PHOTOS AND LET THE CHILDREN COLOR IN THE LIGHT AREAS WITH COLORED PENCILS OR CRAYONS. TELL THEM ABOUT THEIR BELOVED FAMILY MEMBERS AS YOU WORK TOGETHER.

WHAT YOU DO

Choose small frames with holes or spaces in the frames. Spray-paint the frames gold. Allow to dry. Make black and white copies of the desired photos. Reduce or enlarge the photos to fit in the purchased frames. Using colored pencils, color in the light areas of the photos. Color in the same direction in large areas. Frame the photos. String the beads on the wire and secure the ends. Place beaded wire through hole in frame and hang on the tree.

Make use of those wonderful
autumn finds by painting and stringing
them on your holiday tree.

Nature's Garland

 WHAT YOU NEED

Pine cones, nuts, acorns, leaves
  and other found nature items
Drill and ⅛-inch drill bit; awl
Newspaper
Dark red spray paint
Bronze spray paint; toothpick
Large needle; green dental floss

 WHAT YOU DO

Drill holes in nature items, drilling toward one end of the item rather than directly in the middle. This will allow the garland to hang more evenly. Make a hole in the leaves using an awl. Lay the nature items on newspaper and spray lightly with the bronze paint turning the items as needed. Clear the holes with a toothpick. Allow to dry. Lightly spray another layer of dark red paint over the bronze paint. Clear the holes with the toothpick if necessary. Let dry. Thread the needle with the floss. String the garland as desired.

27

Let the light shine through these transparent trims. Fill a tabletop tree in no time with cookie cutter shapes made of wax.

Tiny Wax Motifs

WHAT YOU NEED

Candle wax

Coloring for candles or old colored candles to melt

Small can, saucepan, and heat source for melting wax

Aluminum foil; cookie sheet

Small cookie cutters

Fine glitter in desired colors

Toothpick

Fine silver cord for hanging

WHAT YOU DO

Break up wax and place in can. Place can in pan of water and place on heating source to melt. See *page 15* for wax-melting tips. To color the wax, add desired coloring or old colored candles to the can. Melt the wax only until it is liquid. Remove from heat. Cover cookie sheet with foil. Pour wax on foil. Allow to set until wax is no longer transparent, about five minutes. Using the cookie cutters, cut out desired shapes (see photo, *left*). Make a hole in the top of the shape using a toothpick while the wax is still warm. Dust with glitter. Allow to cool completely. Thread cording through hole to hang. Knot ends.

Sweet Candy Tree

(For the Flower Gumdrop Ornaments)

Large and small gumdrops

White 24-gauge wire

Old scissors or wire cutters

(For the Circle Gumdrop Ornaments)

Small gumdrops

White 24-gauge wire

Old scissors or wire cutters

Waxed paper

Egg white; coarse sugar

(For the Candy Garland)

Purchased candy necklaces

Small white gumdrops

White dental floss; large needle

WHAT YOU DO

Note: When stringing gumdrops, use a damp cloth to wipe the needle or wire, preventing it from becoming too sticky.

(For the Flower Gumdrop Ornaments)

Choose one large gumdrop and seven small ones. Cut six 2-inch-long pieces of wire and one 5-inch-long piece. Push the seven pieces of wire into the large gumdrop like spokes on a wheel. Push the little gumdrops onto the wire; trim extra wire if needed. The long wire goes through the top gumdrop and comes out the other side leaving a long length for a hook.

(For the Circle Gumdrop Ornaments)

Cut a 9-inch length of wire. String gumdrops onto the wire. Twist ends of the wire together leaving a length of wire for a hook. Lay the ornament on the waxed paper; brush with egg white; sprinkle with coarse sugar. Let dry.

(For the Candy Garland)

Cut the candy necklace apart. Thread a large needle with dental floss. Tie a piece of candy at one end; string the white gumdrops and candies as desired. Tie a piece of candy to the end to finish.

A pretty painted flowerpot holds this sweet candy tree topped with a lollipop. Even though the sugary trims are made using real candy, they won't be edible now. So have a bowl of candy nearby for Christmas munching.

Birdie Tree Trims

The birds will enjoy these edible
ornaments made especially for them.
Place on any outdoor tree and
watch the happy birds come visit
for the holidays.

 WHAT YOU NEED

Kiwi

Sharp knife, spoon

Fine twine

Bird seed

Apples

Small star cookie cutter

Peanut butter

 WHAT YOU DO

For the kiwi cups, slice the
kiwi in half and scoop out
the fruit. Use the knife to
poke a hole in each side
and tie the twine in the
holes. Fill with bird seed
and hang on the tree
outside. *For the apple goodies,*
slice the apple in ¼-inch
slices. Using the cookie
cutter, cut the shape from
the middle of the apple.
Spread peanut butter on
the star cutout and the
apple slice. Sprinkle with
bird seed. Poke a hole in
the trims and tie with
twine to hang on the tree.

Thin and delicate, these textured pieces shine in pure white. Made of polymer clay the pieces are textured using around-the-house objects.

Winter Stars

Tracing paper; pencil; scissors

White polymer clay (such as Sculpey)

Rolling tool or rolling pin

Waxed paper; crafts knife (such as an X-acto knife)

Baking sheet; oven

Objects such as buttons, toothpicks, and tools for making texture on the clay (we used a screwdriver, tiny buttons, and the end of a pen)

Fine cording

★ WHAT YOU DO

Enlarge the patterns 200%, *right* and *below left*, trace and cut out. On waxed paper, roll out the clay to approximately ⅛-inch thickness. Cut around the patterns with the crafts knife. Carefully place the stars on the baking sheet. Using buttons, tools, toothpicks or whatever desired, create texture on the front of the stars by gently pressing the object into the clay. Add a hole at the top of each star for hanging. *For the 8-pointed star,* bring every other point to the center and press to hold. Cover the center with a small ball of clay. Texturize the center of the ball.

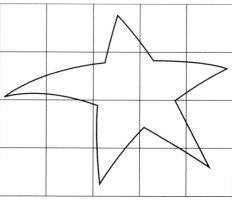

SHOOTING STAR   1 SQUARE = 1 INCH OR ENLARGE AT 200%

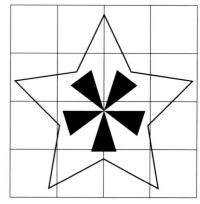

CUT OUT STAR   1 SQUARE = 1 INCH OR ENLARGE AT 200%

For the cut out star, add tiny balls of clay around the cut out area as shown, *opposite.* When the stars are complete, bake following manufacturer's instructions. Allow to cool. Add the cording for hanging.

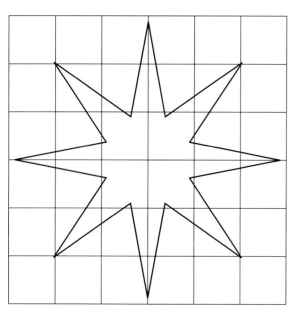

EIGHT-POINTED STAR   1 SQUARE = 1 INCH OR ENLARGE AT 200%

Understated and simple, these coiled trims can be made by the dozens. Fill an entire Christmas tree with the bright colors of the season.

Simply Beaded

MAKE IT TOGETHER

GIVE THE CHILDREN THE BEADS AND CHENILLE STEMS AND YOUR TREE WILL BE FILLED IN NO TIME! THE WHOLE FAMILY WILL HAVE FUN MAKING A HOST OF COLORFUL TRIMS.

WHAT YOU NEED

Metallic chenille stems in
   desired colors
Scissors
Beads with holes just big enough
   to just fit over chenille stems
Pencil

WHAT YOU DO

Cut the chenille stem to an 8-inch length. String the beads on the stem leaving space between the beads. Wrap around a pencil and slide off. Form the chenille stem into a hook at the top of the trim for hanging.

Beads and Paper Garland

Squares of paper and colorful beads combine to make a playful, childlike garland.

 WHAT YOU NEED

1½-inch squares of paper in
   desired colors
Medium-size beads
Large needle
Fine green cording or
   heavy thread

 WHAT YOU DO

Lay the colors of paper and beads out in the order that you wish to string them. Use the needle to poke holes in the center of the papers. Thread the needle with the cording. Tie a bead on the end. Start stringing the papers and beads alternately until the garland is the length desired. Tie a bead at the end to secure.

This shining star seems to look to the heavens. Simply made by covering a star shape with pearls, this beauty will top many a holiday tree.

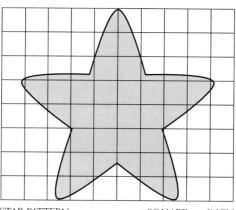

Star of Pearls

WHAT YOU NEED

Tracing paper; pencil; scissors

½-inch sheet of plastic foam (such as Styrofoam)

Sharp knife; thin crafting wire

White duct tape

Bags of pearls (available at crafts stores) or pearls from old necklaces

Tacky crafts glue

WHAT YOU DO

Enlarge the star shape, *below,* and trace onto tracing paper. Cut out and draw onto the plastic foam. Carefully cut it out with a sharp knife. Wrap the

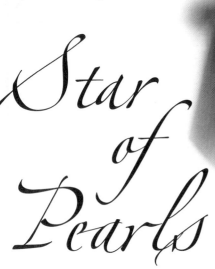

STAR PATTERN   1 SQUARE = 1 INCH
OR ENLARGE TO 400%

crafting wire around the star and twist at back for hanging. Flatten the wire on the front and tape down with white tape. Working on one area at a time, apply the glue generously on the front of the star. (Cover the tape as well as the rest of the front of the star.) Place the pearls on the glue. Fill in the areas with glue and pearls until the entire star and edges are covered. Allow to dry thoroughly before hanging.

More Ideas
for ornaments and garlands

Make it a tradition to give a handmade ornament as a gift to a special person each year. Place the ornament in a square box and wrap in plain-colored paper. Write "starting a new tradition" over and over on the outside of the wrapped box using a gold marking pen. Add a pretty bow to the package.

Try making garlands from favorite candies. String jelly beans, hard candies with holes, gumdrops, and other favorites on waxed dental floss.

Put vintage ornaments in a large crystal glass bowl and display on the center of table resting on a favorite doily or holiday napkin.

Use narrow holiday ribbons instead of ornament hangers to hang the trims on the Christmas tree this year.

Make copies of favorite photos, cut out, and glue to a star-shaped piece of felt for a simple "from the kids" gift.

When giving an ornament as a gift, make a special hanger by stringing beads onto colored wire and attaching it to the ornament.

Make small kitchen tools into ornaments by painting them with acrylic paint and hanging them on a small tree in your kitchen.

Fill small florist bags with goodies and hang them on the tree as holiday ornaments.

Use a starched baby stocking as a gift-holder for money and hang on the tree.

Display favorite round ornaments propped in crystal candlestick holders. Group on a mantel or buffet for a striking effect.

"*Deck the halls with boughs of holly.*"

—Traditional Christmas Carol

illuminate
your
holiday home
with
wreaths
and
centerpieces

Using an unexpected tool to carve these winter fruits yields a lovely and aromatic centerpiece.

Citrus Pomanders

WHAT YOU DO

Choose the desired piece of fruit. With a pencil, mark a dot where you want to carve the stars on the fruit. Using the linoleum cutter and cutting away from yourself, make a star by carving an × at the dot and then making another line through the × once or twice through the middle, forming a star. Continue making stars randomly on the fruits. Push a whole clove in the center of each star. Place several pieces of fruit in a clear glass bowl with cinnamon sticks and fresh greens. This centerpiece will stay fresh for approximately three days.

WHAT YOU NEED

Fresh oranges, lemons, and limes
Pencil
Whole cloves
Linoleum cutter
  (available at crafts
  and discount stores)
Fresh evergreens
Cinnamon sticks

MAKE IT TOGETHER

LET THE CHILDREN PLACE THE CLOVES INTO THE CENTER OF EACH STAR. HAVE A BOWL OF SLICED ORANGES FOR SNACKING WHILE YOU WORK TOGETHER.

Sugar Cube Village

Tiny sugar cubes stack up nicely to create miniature houses, tiny trees, and decorated holiday wreaths. Let the children help create these magical snow-covered wonders.

WHAT YOU NEED

Sugar cubes

Heart sugar cubes from sugar
   cube "Bridge Mix"

Piping Icing (see recipe, opposite)

Waxed paper

Cake decorating bag

Pink jelly beans, green gumdrops,
   "cut rock" candies, and
   assorted other candies as desired

WHAT YOU DO

Place Piping Icing in a disposable decorating bag. Snip tip of bag to make a small opening. To make the houses, *opposite*, work on waxed paper and stack the cubes, piping small amount of icing between each cube. To make a roof

MAKE IT TOGETHER

LET THE LITTLE ONES STACK THE SUGAR CUBES AS YOU PIPE THE FROSTING. WHAT SWEET LITTLE FAVORS YOU WILL MAKE TOGETHER!

section, connect cubes in a rectangle shape. Allow to dry before adding to the house. Add heart sugar cubes on top of house. Attach candy decorations using more icing. To make topiaries, gently reshape green gumdrops into cone shapes. To make the sugar cube trees, *opposite,* arrange a ring of cubes on waxed paper. Add a second ring of cubes on top using icing

to connect the cubes. Continue with smaller rings of cubes until there is a single cube for the top of the tree. Use icing to add edible glitter, sprinkles, or colored sugar. To make the wreath, *opposite,* form a single ring of sugar cubes just so the edges touch. Connect with icing. Pipe a squiggle of icing on top of ring. Sprinkle the wet icing with green sprinkles.

Use dots of icing to attach a few pink candies for berries. Let dry completely.
.

Piping Icing

3 tablespoons meringue powder
6 tablespoons warm water
4 cups sifted powdered sugar

Mix meringue powder and water together until blended. Beat in the powdered sugar until it is a frosting consistency.

Paper Holly Wreath

WHAT YOU NEED

Tracing paper; pencil

9-inch plastic foam wreath
(such as Styrofoam)

Green tissue paper; scissors

Large corsage pin

Short straight pins

Various colors of green solid and
printed cardstock paper (paper
should be green on both sides)

Clear strong crafts glue
(such as E6000)

Small red jingle bells

Tacky crafts glue; fine red glitter

MAKE IT TOGETHER

HAVE A FAVORITE FRIEND
COME OVER FOR
HOT CIDER AND WORK
TOGETHER CUTTING OUT
THE HOLLY LEAVES AS YOU
ARRANGE THEM. THINK
OF ALL THE FUN VISITING
(AND HOLIDAY PLANNING)
YOU CAN DO WHILE
YOU WORK!

WHAT YOU DO

Trace the holly patterns, *below,* onto tracing paper. Trace around each pattern onto the various pieces of solid and patterned green cardstock. You will need about 45 holly leaves in various sizes. Cut out the leaves, bend slightly down the middle; set aside. Cut strips of tissue paper and wrap the wreath form until it is covered, pinning as needed to hold. Using the large corsage pin, poke a hole at the top of each leaf. Group the leaves by threes and pin to the tissue-covered wreath, arranging as desired. When the arrangement is done, gently lift the leaves and secure with glue. Glue the red jingle bells in groups between the leaves. Allow to dry. Dab a little crafts glue on the jingle bells and dust with fine red glitter. Let dry.

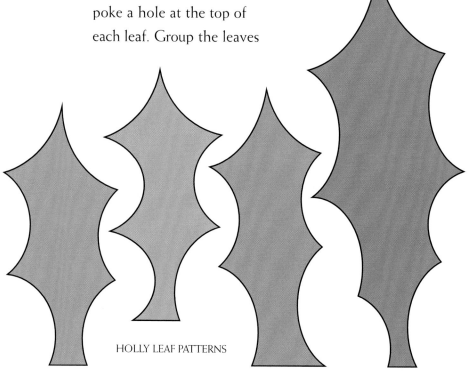

HOLLY LEAF PATTERNS

**Green papers in all shades and
bright red jingle bells form this
holly wreath that welcomes your
holiday guests.**

Winter Green Centerpiece

This elegant centerpiece made of traditional fruit will last season after season dressed in winter green paint and a sparkle of glitter.

WHAT YOU NEED

Small dropcloth

Purchased artificial fruits

Spray paint
  (we used Design
  Master forest green)

Mint green fine glitter

Fresh evergreens

Pedestal dish or bowl

WHAT YOU DO

Lay out the fruits on the dropcloth. Lightly spray paint on one side. Allow to dry. Turn and paint the other side. Allow to dry. Spray the tops and bottoms in the same manner, allowing to dry. Stand the fruits up on the drop cloth and lightly spray once again. While the paint is wet, dust with glitter. Allow to dry. Arrange the fruits in a bowl or pedestal dish with greens.

Vintage Wreath

WHAT YOU NEED

Small Christmas items, such as
    acrylic fruit, Santas, reindeer,
    ornaments, etc.
Newspapers
Primer (such as Kilz) and red
    metallic spray paint (available
    at hobby or crafts stores)
10-inch plastic foam wreath
    form (such as Styrofoam)
Packages of red tinsel garland
Scissors
Short straight pins
Hot-glue gun and glue sticks
¼-inch-wide red satin ribbon
1-inch red muffin cup liners
3-inch-wide red wire edge
    ribbon for bow

WHAT YOU DO

Choose the items you want to put on the wreath (see photo 1). Lay them on the newspaper and paint with primer. Allow to dry. Paint the items with the metallic red paint. Turn the objects and paint again if necessary. Allow to dry. Set aside. Cut the tinsel into 3-foot lengths to make it easier to wrap the form. Starting anywhere on the back side of wreath, pin one end of the tinsel. Start wrapping the wreath until that length of tinsel is used (see photo 2). Add another length and continue until the wreath is entirely wrapped. Pin the end of the tinsel on the back. Hot-glue the painted Christmas items to the tinsel. Make tiny fans by cutting a section from the muffin liners. Poke a hole in the corner and add a ribbon. Hot-glue onto wreath. Tie a bow with the wire-edged ribbon and glue to center of wreath.

What color says Christmas more than beautiful
Christmas red? A little metallic spray paint and
traditional tree tinsel combine with knickknacks
to make this elegantly red holiday statement.

Miniature pineapples and other nature items are painted a shimmering copper color to make this stunning holiday wreath.

Copper Luster Wreath

WHAT YOU NEED

Miniature pineapples (available in the fruit section of grocery stores)

Pine cones

Floral berry sprigs

Floral sticks with wire

20-gauge floral wire and cutters

Metallic copper spray paint

Waxed paper

Purchased green wreath

Copper colored ribbon for bow

WHAT YOU DO

Wrap a piece of wire around the end of each pine cone so it can be wired into the wreath. Place a floral stick with wire into the pineapple. Place the pineapples, pine cones, and sprigs on the waxed paper. Spray with copper paint, turning as necessary. Allow to dry. Arrange the items on the wreath and wire in place. Tie a large ribbon bow and attach to the top of the wreath.

Snowflake Vase

With a simple rubber stamp, a little paint, and fresh flowers you can make a holiday centerpiece.

WHAT YOU NEED

Plastic plate; plastic spoon
Clear glass vase with
 straight sides
Purchased rubber stamp
White or cream colored
 glass paints
Fresh flowers and greens

MAKE IT A GIFT

WHO WOULDN'T LOVE A VASE AS CLEVER AS THIS ONE? SO EASY AND INEXPENSIVE TO MAKE, YOU CAN MAKE ONE FOR THOSE SPECIAL NEIGHBORS OR FOR A FAVORITE TEACHER.

WHAT YOU DO

Be sure the vase is clean and free of fingerprints. Pour a small amount of glass paint onto the plastic plate. Smooth it out with a plastic spoon. Dip the stamp into the paint and press onto the glass vase. Repeat stamping the motif until the desired effect is achieved. Let the paint dry. If necessary, bake according to the manufacturer's instructions. Fill the vase with red or white flowers and fresh greens.

Fragrant Candle Ring

Cuddle up with a cup of spiced cider and enjoy the delightful fragrance of this easy-to-make candle ring.

WHAT YOU NEED

7-inch plastic foam wreath form (such as Styrofoam)

Waxed paper

Tacky crafts glue

Cinnamon sticks

Coffee beans

Coarsely ground coffee

Brown votive candle

Small plate

MAKE IT TONIGHT

TURN ON THE CHRISTMAS MUSIC AND MAKE A POT OF COFFEE AND YOU'LL HAVE THIS CLEVER CANDLE RING FINISHED IN LESS THAN AN HOUR.

WHAT YOU DO

Place the wreath form on the waxed paper. Generously spread the glue on one area of the wreath form and arrange the sticks on the wreath. Glue the coffee beans between the sticks. Continue until the wreath is covered. Spread glue on the sides of the wreath and press on ground coffee. Place wreath on small plate, place candle in center and surround with coffee beans.

Wrapped with ribbon and beads, this lovely centerpiece reflects the sparkle of the vintage ornament collection it holds.

Beribboned Centerpiece

MAKE IT TONIGHT

EVEN IF YOU ONLY HAVE A FEW MINUTES BEFORE YOUR GUESTS ARRIVE, YOU CAN MAKE THIS PROJECT. THEY'RE SURE TO OOH AND AAH OVER YOUR CLEVER CRAFTING TALENT!

WHAT YOU NEED

Glass bowl
Purchased beaded ribbon trim (available at crafts stores)
Strong crafts glue (such as E6000)
Vintage Christmas ornaments

WHAT YOU DO

Position the beaded ribbon on the bowl and glue in place with strong crafts glue. The glue will dry quickly but the ribbon may slide so watch it carefully for a few minutes. Allow to dry and fill bowl with ornaments in coordinating colors.

Holiday Nut Wreath

The warm brown colors of this holiday wreath seem to echo Christmases past. Arrange the nuts however you like mixing textures, sizes, and colors.

 WHAT YOU NEED

Assorted mixed nuts in the shell

Band saw/protective glasses

9-inch plastic foam wreath form
  (such as Styrofoam)

Hot-glue gun and glue sticks

3-inch-wide ribbon for bow

24-gauge copper wire

 WHAT YOU DO

Wearing protective glasses, use a band saw to cut the nuts in the shell in half. If you do not have a band saw, glue the uncut nuts to the wreath form. They will be a little more difficult to glue, but they will stick to one another. (If using the whole nuts, choose ones with flat sides.) After all of the nuts are glued to the wreath form, allow to dry. Tie a bow from the ribbon and wire it around the top of wreath. Use this wire to hang the wreath as well.

Colored seashells with a bit of glue and ribbon are all it takes to make this delightful wreath to use in those hard to decorate rooms.

Seashell Wreath

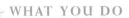

WHAT YOU DO

If using found shells, paint shells in desired colors. Allow to dry. Loop wire around the top of the wreath and secure in the back for hanging. Arrange painted shells on the front of the wreath form as desired, gluing over the wire. Glue small areas at a time. Hot-glue shells along the edges of the wreath as well. Allow to dry. Tie a ribbon bow and hot-glue to the top of the wreath.

WHAT YOU NEED

Purchased 9-inch flat foam
  wreath form (such as Styrofoam)
9-inch piece of fine wire for
  hanger
Painted seashells (available
  pre-painted at crafts and
  discount stores) Note: If using
  found shells, paint as desired
  with acrylic paints
Hot-glue gun and glue sticks
One yard of 3-inch-wide
  wire-edge ribbon

MAKE IT TOGETHER

LET EACH CHILD HAVE A SMALL DISH OF SHELLS. LET THEM
HAND YOU THE TREASURED PIECES AS YOU GLUE THEM ON THE
WREATH. EVERYONE WILL BE PROUD OF THE RESULTS.

Sugared Fruit Tree

Frosted with glistening sugar, this decorative fruit centerpiece brings traditional holiday fruits to the table in a new light.

WHAT YOU NEED

Plastic foam cone (such as Styrofoam)

Clear glass plate

Toothpicks

Small sugar pears; lemon juice

Cranberries

Parsley

Fine and coarse sugar

Egg white; paintbrush

WHAT YOU DO

Place the cone on the plate. Break the toothpicks in half and skewer the fruit. Starting at the bottom of the cone, poke the skewered fruit into the cone. Cut the pears in half if necessary (and dip into lemon juice) to fill the holes. After all of the pears are placed, fill open areas with cranberries and parsley. Brush the entire piece with egg white. Sprinkle with coarse and fine white sugar. Allow to dry. Centerpiece will last approximately 2–3 days.

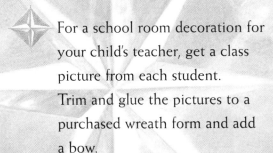

More Ideas
for wreaths and centerpieces

For a school room decoration for your child's teacher, get a class picture from each student. Trim and glue the pictures to a purchased wreath form and add a bow.

Embellish an artificial green wreath by hot-gluing favorite board game pieces such as checkers, chess pieces, or dice to the wreath. Add a bow and hang in the game room.

Make a "choose-a-gift" centerpiece by wrapping tiny gifts and placing them in a large bowl in the center of the table. Let everyone choose a gift for their table favor.

Paint a purchased pine cone wreath with metallic green spray paint for a stunningly simple and very sparkling holiday wreath.

Use an inexpensive rose bowl to float red and white roses with a dusting of glitter for a last-minute holiday centerpiece.

Top a purchased evergreen wreath with a bow tied from a vintage handkerchief. Try to find a hankie with Christmas motifs or in the colors of Christmas.

Hot-glue wrapped red-and-white peppermint Christmas candies to a purchased foam wreath form for a quick and striking wreath.

Make a simple centerpiece by filling a glass bowl with star fruit and fresh greens. Add a few fresh cranberries to complete the holiday look.

Glue colorful Christmas diecuts from the scrapbook store to a purchased wreath form overlapping to cover the form.

"Happy Christmas to all and to all a good night!"

—A VISIT FROM ST. NICHOLAS (1823)

make your
greetings
shine
with
**handmade
cards**

Christmas Wishes

WHAT YOU NEED

Tracing paper; pencil

5¼×8½-inch piece of cream tone-on-tone paper

Red vellum paper

Lime green scrapbook paper

Fine-line gold marking pen

Scissors; tacky crafts glue

Rubber stamp with Christmas greeting and gold stamp pad

4⅝×5¾-inch piece of gold metallic cardstock

Purchased red envelope

Scraps of gold cardstock

Decorative scissors

WHAT YOU DO

Score and fold the cream paper in half. Trace the patterns, *below,* onto tracing paper and cut out. Cut two flowers from each pattern and the three circles from the red vellum paper. Layer and glue the two largest flowers together just in the middle, curling up the petals. Do the same for the medium and the small flowers. Glue the layered flowers onto the card front. Glue the circles to the center of each flower. Embellish the centers using the fine line gold pen. Cut eight leaf patterns from the lime green cardstock. Tuck and glue the leaves under the flowers. Stamp the Christmas greeting on the bottom front of the card. Glue the back of the finished card to the single piece of gold cardstock. Use the decorative scissors to cut a strip of gold cardstock and glue it to the envelope flap.

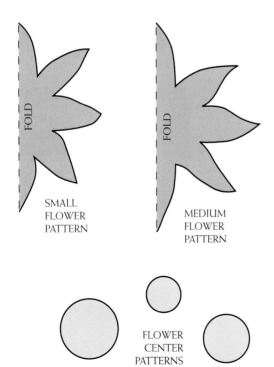

SMALL FLOWER PATTERN

FOLD

MEDIUM FLOWER PATTERN

FOLD

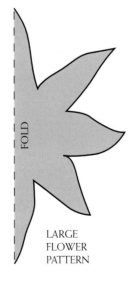

FOLD

LARGE FLOWER PATTERN

FLOWER CENTER PATTERNS

LEAF PATTERN

Poinsettias that stand up and convey
"Christmas Wishes" make this pretty
card one that is sure to be displayed
year after year.

Shake it gently like a treasured snow globe and this card makes its own holiday fun. Purchased confetti fills the magic acetate ball.

Snow Globe Card

WHAT YOU NEED

6×9-inch piece of white
  cardstock; crafts knife
3½×7-inch piece of clear acetate
6×4½-inch piece of white cardstock
Christmas confetti
Transparent tape; crafts glue
Green glitter sticky back paper
  (available at crafts stores)
Silver cording

WHAT YOU DO

Score and fold the 6×9-inch piece of white cardstock in half. Using the crafts knife, cut a 2¼-inch circle in center front of card. Fold the acetate in half. Seal two sides with tape forming a pocket. Place confetti into open end of pocket. Seal with tape. Tape the acetate pocket to inside front of the card. Glue the 6×4½-inch piece of white cardstock over pocket. Glue silver cord around the outside edge of the globe on card front. Write JOY with crafts glue; place cord over glue to form the word. Cut a 2×1½-inch rectangle from the glitter paper. Angle the top and stick at globe base. Decorate envelope flap with silver cording.

For the tag

Cut a rectangle from green cardstock. Center a smaller rectangle of green glitter paper in the center. Glue cording around the edge. Tie a small bow from cording; glue to corner of tag as shown.

Contemporary Card

Sometimes simple shapes can make the most impressive statement. Add a clever sticker and your greeting is complete.

MAKE IT TONIGHT

You can create a whole set of these cards in an evening. The inside message could say "May Simple Joys be Yours" or "May Your Christmas be Jolly".

WHAT YOU NEED

5½×11-inch piece of white
   cardstock
1½-inch colored cardstock
   squares or circles (we used
   purchased precut shapes)
Glue stick; purchased 3-D sticker

WHAT YOU DO

Score and fold the white cardstock in half. Arrange squares (or circles) evenly on the front of the card. Use glue stick to adhere shapes in place. Place a sticker on the center shape.

For the tag
Overlap and glue three squares in a row; punch one end. Glue a circle on top; use a metallic pen for lettering.

Antique-Look Greetings

Color copies of postcards sent long ago send warm holiday greetings today. Use the vintage art provided on page 187, or search antiques stores for more inspirations.

WHAT YOU NEED

Photocopy of desired image

Scissors

Ruler; scoring tool

9×6½-inch pieces of cardstock
  in desired colors

Narrow ribbon

Clear crafts glue

Fine glitter

Paper punch

8×11-inch piece of lightweight
  patterned paper to match
  color of card for envelope

Scraps of colored cardstock
  for tag

Metallic marking pen

WHAT YOU DO

Color copy or scan the desired postcard or image onto cardstock *(see page 187)*. Trim and set aside. Score and fold the colored cardstock in half. Center and glue the copied image to the front of card. Make a fine line of glue around the image. Dust with glitter. Punch two holes or any even number of holes along the folded edge of the card. Thread the ribbon through the holes; tie a bow. *To make the envelope,* lay the lightweight paper with a short end up. Score the top 1-inch of the paper. Fold to the inside forming a flap. Angle the edges. Score and fold the bottom 10 inches in half. The envelope should now

measure 8×5 inches when
folded. Open the paper
and with the top flap lying
flat, score and fold ½-inch
in at each side; glue front
and back together. The
final envelope should
measure 7×5 inches.

For the tags
Color copy or scan the
images on *page 187* onto
cardstock. Using small
scissors, cut out small areas
to be used. We used the
holly, wreath, and Santa
areas. Cut small squares

from colored cardstock.
Glue trimmed images to
colored paper. Punch a
hole in corner; add a
ribbon. Use a metallic
marker for lettering.

Make a handmade card to include a gift that will always be remembered.

Gifted Greeting

WHAT YOU NEED

5¼×5¼-inch
  piece of green cardstock
5×5-inch piece of red cardstock
Purchased 4-inch vellum
  envelope
Crafts glue
Gold paint marking pen
Paper punch
10 inches of gold cording
Scissors; pinking shears
Vintage handkerchief
Purchased green envelope

WHAT YOU DO

Glue the red cardstock on the green cardstock. Cut the top off the vellum envelope using pinking shears. Write "A Gift for You!" using the gold marking pen. Color the top edge of the vellum using the gold marking pen. Glue the side and bottom edges of the vellum envelope on the red cardstock. Punch a hole at the top two corners of the card. Knot one end of the cord and pull through the punched hole to the other side. Knot the other end of the cord. Write "Merry Christmas!" at the bottom of the card with the gold pen. Fold and tuck the hankie into the vellum envelope. Trim the edge of the green envelope with decorative scissors; color the flap edge with the gold paint marker.

Poinsettia Leaves Card

Share a beautiful fresh poinsettia by color-copying the leaves and reassembling them onto a holiday greeting to send to a dear friend.

WHAT YOU NEED

Red and pink cardstock

10×5-inch piece of white cardstock

Real poinsettia leaves; scissors

Glue stick; tacky crafts glue

Gold micro beads

Purchased red envelope

Gold paint marking pen

WHAT YOU DO

Carefully snip a few small leaves from your holiday poinsettia. Take them to the copy shop and have them color copied onto red or pink cardstock. Cut out the leaves. Set them aside. Score and fold the white cardstock in half. Use a glue stick to glue the copied leaves onto the front of the folded card. Using the tacky crafts glue, make a large circle in the center of the leaves. Sprinkle with micro beads. Allow to dry. Embellish the flap of the envelope with a gold marking pen.

Jingling Snowman

This jolly fellow brings along a little jingle bell song with his magic holiday greeting.

WHAT YOU NEED

Tracing paper; pencil; scissors

8×10-inch piece of blue cardstock

Scraps of white, black, and
   orange cardstock

Glue stick

Marking pens in red and black

Purchased felt self-stick stars

Red sticky-back felt

Red chenille stem

Three small jingle bells

4-inch piece of cord or string

MAKE IT TOGETHER

LET THE CHILDREN HELP "BUILD" THIS SNOWMAN BY LETTING THEM CUT THE CIRCLE SHAPES FOR THE BODY. THE SNOWMAN SHAPE WILL TAKE ON A VERY CHILDLIKE AND REALISTIC LOOK.

WHAT YOU DO

Score and fold blue cardstock in half. Cut a 2-inch, a 1½-inch, and a 1-inch circle from white cardstock. Set aside. Trace the hat and nose patterns, *below.* Cut out. Cut hat from black and nose from orange cardstock. Cut a ½×1½-inch scarf from red felt. Fringe the end. Assemble snowman and glue with glue stick. Poke a hole at each side of the snowman. Thread chenille stem through holes. Draw eyes, mouth and buttons using marking pen. Stick the stars to the background. Thread the jingle bells on the cording; attach to chenille stem by pinching the ends. Inside message could say, "Jingle all the Way this Christmas" or "May your Days be Merry and Bright."

HAT AND NOSE PATTERNS

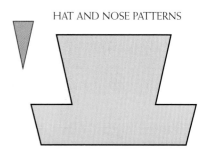

Golden Greeting

Golden cross-stitch paper brings life into this tree adorned with colorful jewels and an appliqué topper.

WHAT YOU NEED

Tracing paper; pencil; scissors
3¾×5½-inch piece of green cardstock; crafts knife
6¾×10-inch piece of red cardstock
4¼×6-inch piece of metallic

gold cross-stitch paper (available at crafts stores)
Round jewels in desired sizes and colors; tacky crafts glue
Star appliqué; one star jewel
Three diamond or oval jewels
Purchased envelope

WHAT YOU DO

Trace the tree pattern, *below*, onto tracing paper and cut out. Draw around the pattern onto green paper. Cut out with the crafts knife. Set aside. Score and fold the red cardstock in half. Center and glue the gold paper to the front of the card. Center and glue the green paper with the tree cut out atop the gold paper. Glue round jewels on tree and star appliqué and jewel at the top. Glue diamond jewels at base of tree. Add two round jewels at each corner of the card. Trim envelope flap with jewels.

TREE PATTERN

Reminiscent of the images seen on the cards of the 1950s, this simple card will bring a smile to the one who receives it.

Glittering Message

ORNAMENT
TOPPER PATTERN

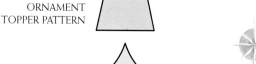

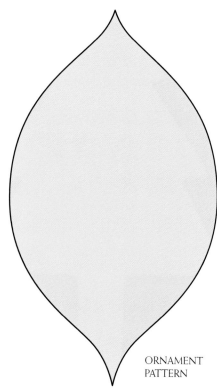

ORNAMENT
PATTERN

WHAT YOU NEED

9×5-inch piece of dark red polka dot cardstock

Star image rubber stamp

Metallic gold stamp pad

Tracing paper; pencil

Scissors

Small piece of gold cardstock

Scrap of sticky-back gold glitter paper

Gold paper scraps

Gold glitter paint

Glue stick

WHAT YOU DO

Score and fold the dark red cardstock in half. Using the rubber stamp, stamp stars on front of card. Let dry. Trace the patterns, *left*, onto tracing paper; cut out. Cut the ornament shape from gold cardstock. Decorate with paper scraps and gold glitter as desired. Cut the topper from a scrap of gold glitter paper. Glue the ornament to the front of the card using the glue stick. Place the topper at the top of the ornament.

More Ideas
for handmade cards

 Create a card that features your child's original artwork. Let your child draw on a piece of 4×6-inch cardstock using crayons or markers. After the art is completed, glue it to a folded card with a 5×7-inch front. Embellish around the edges with a bit of rubber stamping or tiny colored buttons.

 Old photos make wonderful images on the front of greeting cards. Color-copy the photos and adhere to the front of a folded piece of cardstock. Don't be afraid to use the ones that feature you as a teenager!

 Make a keepsake card by embellishing the front of the card with a small piece of cross-stitch that you have created. Fringe the edges before you attach it to the front of the card. Sign and date the card.

 Purchase a simple greeting card and make it your own by adding a bit of glue and glitter to solid areas of color. Sign your name using a glitter pen and write "sparkle added by _____."

 To make a clever card for giving money, use decorative scissors to cut off the top of a small colored envelope. Decorate it with metallic markers. Glue it to the front of your blank card. Fold the money and slide it inside the envelope pocket.

 Make your family photo the focus of your greeting card this year. Have the photo taken in black and white and have everyone wear solid light-colored clothing. Using colored pencils, color in areas or draw tiny holiday prints on the plain light areas of the photo. Mount the photo on black paper and attach it to the front of the card.

"Christmas is coming,
the geese are getting fat."

—BEGGAR RHYME

create
some
shimmering
holiday
goodies
from
your
kitchen

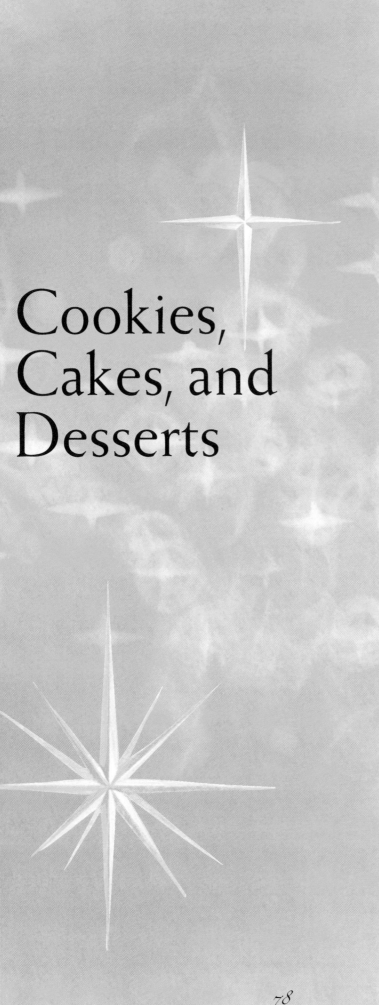

Cookies, Cakes, and Desserts

WHAT YOU NEED

For the base crust

- ½ cup butter, softened
- 2 tablespoons powdered sugar
- 2 tablespoons granulated sugar
- 1 cup flour

For the filling

- 2 eggs, beaten
- 2 tablespoons lemon juice
  Grated rind of one lemon
- 1 cup granulated sugar
- 2 tablespoons flour
- ½ teaspoon baking powder

WHAT YOU DO

For the base crust, in a small bowl, mix together all *base crust* ingredients and press into a greased 8-inch square pan. Bake in a 350° oven for 12 minutes. Set aside. *For the filling*, in a small bowl mix all *filling* ingredients and pour onto prepared crust. Bake 25 minutes more. Cool slightly. Drizzle with Powdered Sugar Glaze. Dust with powdered sugar. Cool in refrigerator before cutting with star cookie cutters. Makes 16 bars or 12 various size stars.

Powdered Sugar Glaze

- 1 cup powdered sugar
- 1 tablespoon milk

Beat until smooth.

Lemon Star Bars

Like the stars in the sky above,
these delightful stars may all disappear
before morning!

Shaped and sparkling like winter snowflakes, these crispy cookies are all unique and elegant—delicious to eat, yet beautiful enough to give as a simple gift.

Snowflake Sugar Cookies

WHAT YOU NEED

- ½ cup butter, softened
- 1 cup granulated sugar
- ½ teaspoon lemon flavoring
- ½ teaspoon vanilla
- 2 eggs
- 1 teaspoon baking soda dissolved in ¼ cup hot milk
- 2¾ cups flour
- 1½ teaspoon cream of tartar
- 3-inch snowflake cookie cutters (see sources, page 191)

MAKE IT A GIFT

FOLD AN 8-INCH PAPER DOILY IN HALF, AND IN HALF AGAIN. WRITE THE NAME WITH A GOLD MARKER ON THE DOILY FRONT. PAPER PUNCH THE CORNER AND TIE ON A SMALL JINGLE BELL WITH THE RIBBON. TUCK A SNOWFLAKE COOKIE (OR TWO) BETWEEN THE DOILY FOLDS.

WHAT YOU DO

In a mixing bowl, cream butter, sugar, flavorings, and eggs. Add soda dissolved in hot milk and dry ingredients. Mix well. Roll out to ¼-inch thickness and cut with snowflake cookie cutter. Place on greased cookie sheet and sprinkle with sugar if desired or leave plain to frost. Bake in a 325° oven for 10 minutes. Remove carefully from pan. Frost with Simple Icing if desired (see page 94). Yields 2 dozen cookies.

The colors of Christmas are rolled together to create this colorful holiday dessert.

Pretty Cake Roll

WHAT YOU NEED

Parchment paper
One box angel food cake mix
Clean white cloth larger
  than a jelly roll pan
  (such as a dishtowel)
½ cup powdered sugar
Red food coloring
Pistachio ice cream

WHAT YOU DO

Preheat oven to 350°. Line a 15×10-inch jelly roll pan with parchment paper. Do not grease. Paper will extend above pan edge. Prepare the cloth by laying it flat and dusting it with powdered sugar; set aside. Prepare cake mix according to package directions, using red food coloring to tint the cake. Pour batter into prepared jelly roll pan. Bake 16 to 18 minutes. Top will be slightly brown and edges will be slightly cracked. The cake should spring back when touched. Cool on rack 10 minutes. Turn out onto prepared cloth. Remove parchment. Roll cake and towel together from long side. Let cool. Carefully unroll cake. Remove towel. Spread ice cream about 1 inch thick to within ½ inch of edge. Reroll cake. Freeze until firm. To serve, cut into 1½-inch slices. Serves 10.

Wafer Treats

These tiny treats are so rich that you'll want to eat them like candy. Add some to a cookie tray or serve them with cherry nut ice cream for a simple dessert.

WHAT YOU NEED

1 cup butter, softened

⅓ cup whipping cream

2 cups flour, sifted

   Granulated sugar for dipping

1 recipe Holiday Frosting

WHAT YOU DO

In a small bowl combine softened butter and whipping cream. Add the flour; mix well and chill 1 to 2 hours. Roll dough to ¼-inch thickness on floured board. Cut with a 1-inch round cookie cutter. Dip into granulated sugar. Place cookies on an ungreased cookie sheet; prick with a fork 4 times. Bake in 370° oven for 7 to 9 minutes. When cooled, frost with Holiday Frosting, stacking sandwich-style. Makes 70 cookies.

Holiday Frosting

¼ cup butter, softened

1 cup powdered sugar

1 teaspoon vanilla

   Cream (about 1 tablespoon)

   Red or green food coloring

Combine all ingredients adding just enough cream to make a stiff frosting. Tint with red or green food coloring.

MAKE IT A GIFT

TUCK THESE LITTLE COOKIES INTO CANDY HOLDERS AND PLACE IN A BOX FOR A MUCH-LOVED GIFT.

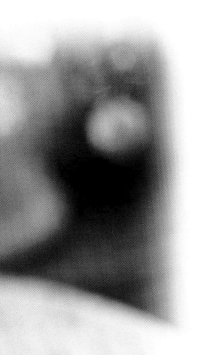

 WHAT YOU NEED

- 3 cups flour
- 2 cups sugar
- 6 tablespoons cocoa
- 1 teaspoon salt
- 2 teaspoons soda
- 2 tablespoons vinegar
- 2 teaspoons vanilla
- ½ cup butter, melted
- 2 cups cold water
- 1 recipe Creamy Chocolate Frosting

Old-Fashioned Chocolate Cake

This no-egg, brownie-like cake is sure to be your family's favorite. It is stirred up in just one large mixing bowl.

 WHAT YOU DO

In a large mixing bowl, mix together the dry ingredients; make a well in the middle. Combine vinegar, vanilla, and butter; add to dry ingredients. Mix well. Add 2 cups cold water and beat well. Pour into ungreased 9×13-inch pan or two 9-inch round pans. Bake in a 350° oven 30 minutes for large pan; 20 minutes for layers. Top with Creamy Chocolate Frosting.

Creamy Chocolate Frosting

- ½ cup butter
- 1½ cups sugar
- 6 Tablespoons milk
- ½ cup light corn syrup
- 1½ cups chocolate chips

In heavy saucepan, combine first four ingredients and bring to a boil. Boil for 2 minutes. Remove from heat; stir in chocolate chips. Stir until all the chips are melted. Cool until spreadable. Frost cake.

Decorated with bits of candy in
beautiful pastels, these cookies can
hang on the tree as decorations or
be enjoyed as an artful treat.

Beautiful Ornament Cookies

WHAT YOU NEED

½ cup butter, softened

1 cup sugar

½ teaspoon salt

1 tablespoon baking powder

¼ teaspoon baking soda

1 egg

¼ cup milk

2 teaspoons vanilla

2¼ cups flour

Ornament shaped cookie cutters (see sources on page 191)

Drinking straw

1 recipe Simple Icing (see page 94)

WHAT YOU DO

In a mixing bowl, cream butter, sugar, salt, baking powder, and baking soda. Beat in egg, milk, vanilla, and flour. Chill for at least 3 hours. On a floured surface, roll to ¼-inch thickness. Cut with cookie cutters. Use a drinking straw to make hole in top of cookie for hanging if desired. Bake in a 375° oven for about 6 to 8 minutes. Remove from oven before edges brown; do not overbake. Frost with Simple Icing. Decorate with candies, dragées, colored sugars, and piped frosting as desired, referring to photos for ideas. Add ribbon if hanging as an ornament. Makes 24 cookies.

Pineapple and spices combine to make these soft cookies perfect for holiday entertaining.

Pineapple Drops

WHAT YOU NEED

1 cup butter, softened

1 cup granulated sugar

½ cup packed brown sugar

1 egg

1 cup drained, crushed pineapple

½ cup pineapple juice

3½ cups flour

1 teaspoon baking soda

¼ teaspoon nutmeg

½ cup chopped nuts

1 recipe Nutty Icing

WHAT YOU DO

In a mixing bowl, cream butter, sugars, and egg. Add pineapple and juice. Mix well. Stir together dry ingredients and add to creamed mixture. Add nuts. Mix well. Chill at least 1 hour. Drop by teaspoonfuls onto greased cookie sheet.

Bake in a 350° oven for 10 minutes. Frost with Nutty Icing. Makes 48 cookies.

Nutty Icing

⅓ cup butter, softened

3 cups sifted powdered sugar

3 tablespoons milk

1 teaspoon clear vanilla

¼ teaspoon salt

2 tablespoons ground nuts

Cream butter and 1 cup of the powdered sugar. Add milk, vanilla, salt, and nuts. Continue adding powdered sugar until frosting consistency.

MAKE IT A GIFT

CUT A 7X7-INCH SQUARE OF CLEAR CELLOPHANE AND LAY THREE COOKIES IN THE CENTER. ROLL THE CELLOPHANE AROUND THE COOKIES AND TIE BOTH ENDS WITH HOLIDAY RIBBON.

Sparkling Sandwich Cookies

These purchased cookies are all dressed up with just a little frosting and a sprinkle of edible glitter.

WHAT YOU NEED

Purchased white frosting in a tube

Purchased white chocolate covered cookies (such as Oreos)

White edible glitter (see sources on page 191)

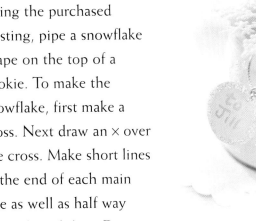

WHAT YOU DO

Using the purchased frosting, pipe a snowflake shape on the top of a cookie. To make the snowflake, first make a cross. Next draw an × over the cross. Make short lines at the end of each main line as well as half way through each line. Dust with edible glitter. Let dry.

MAKE IT A GIFT

THESE COOKIES CAN BE MADE BY THE DOZENS IN AN EVENING SO YOU CAN MAKE PLENTY FOR GIFTS. TO MAKE THE GIFT CONTAINER, USE AN EMPTY POTATO CHIP CAN OR BAKING POWDER CAN WITH A PLASTIC LID. COVER THE OUTSIDE OF THE CAN WITH WHITE PAPER. DRAW SNOWFLAKES ON THE CAN WITH GLUE, AND DUST WITH WHITE GLITTER. GLUE A PURCHASED PLASTIC SNOWFLAKE TO THE LID. FILL THE CAN WITH COOKIES.

Soft, spicy, and oh-so-delicious with a big cup of coffee, these cookies are perfect for Santa on the the big night.

Big Ginger Cookies

WHAT YOU NEED

- ¾ cup butter, softened
- 1 cup sugar
- 1 egg
- ¼ cup molasses
- 2¼ cups flour
- 2 teaspoons ginger
- 1 teaspoon baking soda
- ¾ teaspoon cinnamon
- ½ teaspoon cloves
- ¼ teaspoon salt
- Milk
- 2 tablespoons sugar

MAKE IT A GIFT

DECORATE A PLAIN PAPER SACK BY RUBBER STAMPING A HOLIDAY DESIGN WITH COPPER-COLORED INK. ROLL THE TOP OF THE SACK BACK AND PUNCH WITH A PAPER PUNCH. THREAD A RIBBON THROUGH THE HOLES AND FILL THE SACK WITH GINGER COOKIES.

WHAT YOU DO

In a mixing bowl cream butter, 1 cup sugar, egg, and molasses. Add dry ingredients. Mix well. Shape into 1½-inch balls. Roll in milk and then in the 2 tablespoons sugar. Bake on ungreased cookie sheet in a 350° oven about 10 to 12 minutes, or until lightly browned and still puffed. Do not overbake. Let stand on the cookie sheet for 2 minutes before moving to wire rack. Makes 24 cookies.

Peanut Cakes

WHAT YOU NEED

- 6 egg yolks
- 1 cup sugar
- ½ cup boiling water
- 2 teaspoons vanilla
- 1 tablespoon frozen orange juice concentrate
- 1¾ cup cake flour
- 2¼ teaspoons baking powder
- ½ teaspoon salt
- 20 ounces salted, roasted peanuts, ground
- 1 recipe Butter Frosting

WHAT YOU DO

In a mixing bowl, beat egg yolks until thick and light in color, about 5 minutes. Add sugar. Slowly add boiling water, vanilla, and orange juice. Stir dry ingredients into egg mixture and beat with

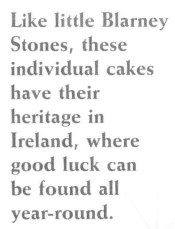

Like little Blarney Stones, these individual cakes have their heritage in Ireland, where good luck can be found all year-round.

mixer for about 2 minutes. Pour batter into greased 9×13-inch baking pan. Bake in a 350° oven for 20 minutes or until toothpick inserted in center comes out clean. Cool. Cut cake into 30 pieces. Remove the brown crust on any edges. Frost each piece on all sides with Butter Frosting. Roll in ground peanuts.

Butter Frosting

- ½ cup butter, softened
- 4½ cups sifted powdered sugar
- ¼ cup milk
- ¼ teaspoon salt
- 1 teaspoon vanilla

In mixing bowl, cream butter and 2 cups of the powdered sugar. Add milk, salt, and vanilla. Beat in more powdered sugar until frosting consistency.

Christmas Tree Cake

WHAT YOU NEED

3 recipes of any 2-layer cake
   mix or cake recipe
1 6-inch square cake pan
1 8-inch square cake pan
3 recipes Decorator Frosting,
   tinted pastel green
   (see page 94)
   Plastic drinking straws
   Decorating bag, coupler
   and round tips
   Assorted silver dragées
   (round and oval)
   (see sources page 191)
1 baked Stained Glass
   Window cookie
   (see page 94)
   Simple Icing (see page 94)

WHAT YOU DO

To prepare cakes, grease cake pans; line bottoms with waxed paper. With each 2-layer cake recipe, bake one 6-inch cake and one 8-inch cake. Bake according to package directions. Stack two of the 6-inch cakes together, spreading some of the Decorator Frosting between layers. Stack two of the 8-inch cakes together spreading frosting between. Stack the last two cakes together (one 6-inch and one 8-inch) spreading frosting between. Trim the last set of cakes to 4×4 inches. To make the cakes an octagonal shape, trim the 4 corners of cakes, making 8 equal sides. Prepare a foil-covered piece of cardboard, trimmed to the exact size and shape of each cake. Place cakes on the boards. To support the cakes, trim 5 drinking straws to height of bottom cake. Each straw should be exactly the same length. Insert the straws down through the top of the cake. Repeat for the middle layer. *Note:* Remove straws before serving. Stack the cakes. To frost cakes, place 1 recipe of the frosting in a mixing bowl. Add enough milk to make frosting slightly thinner so that it spreads very easily. Spread a thin layer of this frosting over the cake. This will prevent crumbs. Let stand a few

continued on page 94

Create a cake to be
the center of attention—
a Christmas Tree! Top
it off with a magic
star cookie.

wet icing. Let dry
completely. Place at top
of cake.

Decorator Frosting

¾ cup butter, softened
4½ cups sifted powdered sugar
3 tablespoons milk
1 teaspoon clear vanilla
½ teaspoon salt

minutes until slightly dry.
Using original consistency
frosting, spread a second
layer over all sides and
tops of octagon cakes.
Make frosting appear
smooth using a long metal
spatula. Place remaining
frosting in a decorating
bag fitted with a coupler
and medium to large sized
round tip. Pipe garlands
and borders on the cakes.
Add silver dragées to the
frosting decorations while
the frosting is still wet.
*To make Stained Glass Window
Cookie,* roll out a favorite
sugar cookie recipe
(*see page 81*) to ¼-inch
thickness. With a large

star cutter, cut out cookie;
place on a foil-lined cookie
sheet. Using a small star
cutter, cut out a star shape
from center of cookie.
Sprinkle some coarsely
crushed, clear hard candy
into the star cut-out. Bake
cookies in a 375° oven for
about 6 minutes or just
until cookie is done. Cool
completely on the foil.
When cool, peel foil
from back of cookie. To
decorate cookie, prepare
Simple Icing. Tint desired
color with food coloring.
With a clean artist's brush,
brush the icing onto the
cookie dough part of
cookie. Add dragées on

In a mixing bowl, mix
butter, vanilla, salt, milk
and *half* of the powdered
sugar. Continue adding
powdered sugar until it
is desired frosting
consistency. Frosts one
2-layer cake recipe.

Simple Icing

⅓ cup water
3 tablespoons meringue powder
4½ cups sifted powdered sugar

In a mixing bowl mix
meringue powder and
water. Add powdered
sugar gradually. Continue
mixing on high speed for
7 to 10 minutes until
fluffy. Makes 3 cups.

Rich and chewy, these beautiful little cookies dress up any holiday cookie plate.

Coconut Gems

WHAT YOU NEED

For the base crust

½ cup butter, softened

¼ cup sugar

1¼ cups flour

For the filling

1 cup well-drained, crushed pineapple

1 egg

½ cup sugar

1 tablespoon butter, softened

2 teaspoons cornstarch

1½ cups flaked coconut

¼ cup chopped pecans

red and green gumdrops (optional)

WHAT YOU DO

In a bowl, mix the *base crust* ingredients together; press into greased 9-inch square pan. Prick with fork. Bake in a 350° oven for 12 minutes. Spread pineapple over crust. Mix remaining ingredients and spread over pineapple. Bake 20 minutes or until browned. Cool. Cut into squares or triangle wedges. Decorate the tops with red and green gumdrops cut into holly shapes if desired. Makes 16 bars.

Covered in pastel sugars, these delightfully rich cookies melt in your mouth.

Snowball Cookies

WHAT YOU NEED

1 cup oil

1 cup butter, softened

1 cup powdered sugar

1 cup granulated sugar

2 eggs

5 cups flour

1 teaspoon cream of tartar

1 teaspoon baking soda

1 teaspoon vanilla or almond
  extract

Coarse pastel colored sugars

WHAT YOU DO

In a mixing bowl, cream the oil, butter, sugars and eggs. Add the flour, cream of tartar, soda, and flavoring. Mix well.

Roll the dough into 1-inch balls. Dip the tops in coarse pastel colored sugar. Place the sugar side up on a greased baking sheet. Bake in a 350° oven for about 10 to 12 minutes. Makes 6 dozen cookies. These cookies will freeze well for up to 3 months.

Candied Tassies

The candied cherries in these tiny goodies glisten, making this already favorite cookie a real beauty.

WHAT YOU NEED

For the base crust

- 1 cup butter
- 2 3-ounce packages cream cheese
- 2 cups flour

For the filling

- 2 eggs
- 1½ cups brown sugar
- 2 tablespoons butter, melted
- ½ teaspoon vanilla
- ¼ teaspoon salt
- 1 cup pecans
- ¾ cup candied cherries

WHAT YOU DO

For the base crust, in a bowl, combine butter and cream cheese until creamy. Add the 2 cups flour, ¼ cup at a time, blending well after each addition. Work with fingers until dough is smooth and well blended. Chill for one hour. Pinch off a small piece of dough and shape into a 1¼-inch ball. Place each ball in a 1¾-inch muffin cup, and with thumb press dough evenly against bottom and sides of cup. Set aside.
For filling, in a bowl beat 2 eggs just enough to mix whites and yolks. Gradually add the brown sugar, beating well. Add the melted butter, vanilla and salt. Mix well. Break a pecan in half and place half on the crust. Spoon filling into cup, filling about ¾ full. Put ½ pecan and candied cherry on top. Bake in a 325° oven for 25 minutes, or until filling is almost set. Let set in pan until almost cool, about 20 minutes, before removing from pan. Makes 3 dozen cookies.

This simple cake is sure to become a holiday tradition. Serve with a red cherry topping, or slice it and serve with Christmas tea.

Mattie's Pound Cake

 WHAT YOU NEED

1¾ cups sugar

1 cup butter

6 eggs

1 teaspoon vanilla

2 cups flour

½ teaspoon salt

 WHAT YOU DO

With a mixer, cream sugar and butter. Add eggs, one at a time, beating thoroughly on high speed after each addition. Add vanilla, flour, and salt, and mix at moderate speed until light and fluffy. Pour into a well-greased, fluted tube pan and bake in a 300° oven for 45 minutes. Raise oven temperature to 315° and bake for an additional 15 minutes, or until a toothpick inserted in the cake comes out clean. Immediately turn out cake onto a cooling rack. Serve with desired topping.

Swedish Lace Cookies

 WHAT YOU NEED

- ¼ cup butter
- ½ cup sugar
- ¾ cup quick oatmeal
- ¼ cup flour
- 2 tablespoons light cream

 WHAT YOU DO

Melt butter. Add all other ingredients. Cook until just bubbly, stirring constantly. Remove from heat. Drop by rounded teaspoonfuls 4 inches apart on a well-greased baking sheet. Flatten slightly with spoon. Bake four at a time in a 375° oven on middle rack for 5 to 6 minutes or until brown around the edges. Cool for 2 minutes before removing from pan. Turn small tumbler upside down and drape cookie over the glass. Let cool. Carefully remove cookie. Invert and fill with berries and whipped cream. Makes twelve 5-inch cookies.

So delicate, this delicious cookie is made to cradle a filling or to eat alone. Serve this lacy treat on Christmas Eve with berries and whipped cream.

Breads, Soups, and Main Dishes

- 1 cup packed brown sugar
- ¼ cup butter, melted
- ¼ cup light corn syrup
- ¼ cup light cream
- 2 cups warm water
- 2 packages dry yeast
- ½ cup butter, melted
- ⅓ cup sugar
- 1 tablespoon salt
- 1 egg
- 6 to 6½ cups flour
- ½ cup dried cherries

WHAT YOU DO

Grease a 9×13-inch cake pan. Combine the first four ingredients; pour into bottom of pan. Set aside. Put warm water into large mixing bowl. Dissolve yeast in water. Add ½ cup butter, sugar, and salt. Beat egg and add to mixture. Add 2 cups of the flour; beat thoroughly. Let rest for five minutes. Gradually add remaining flour and mix. Turn out onto floured surface and knead until smooth. Place back in bowl; cover and let rise until double in bulk. Roll out dough into 12×16-inch rectangle. Spread with a mixture of ½ cup softened butter, ¾ cup sugar and 1 tablespoon cinnamon. Add dried cherries. Roll

Christmas Morning Sticky Rolls

up and slice 1½ inches thick and lay in prepared cake pan. Bake in a 350° oven for about 30 minutes, or until bubbly and brown. Invert onto foil. Cool slightly before serving. Decorate with candied cherries if desired. Makes about 16 large rolls.

They'll be all smiles when you present them with this all-time favorite breakfast treat.

Lizzie's Banana Bread

An old-time favorite, these golden loaves of rich banana flavor make great gifts.

WHAT YOU NEED

- 1 cup sugar
- ½ cup butter, softened
- 2 eggs
- 3 ripe bananas, mashed
- 1 teaspoon baking powder
- 1 teaspoon baking soda
- ¼ teaspoon salt
- 3 tablespoons buttermilk
- 2 cups flour

MAKE IT TOGETHER

LET THE CHILDREN MASH THE BANANAS ON A PLATE USING A DINNER FORK. THIS IS A GREAT WAY TO GET THE LITTLE ONES INTERESTED IN COOKING WITH YOU IN THE KITCHEN.

WHAT YOU DO

In a mixing bowl, cream sugar and butter; add eggs and mashed bananas. Mix baking powder, baking soda, and salt with the buttermilk and add to the creamed mixture. Stir together. Add the 2 cups flour and mix well. Pour into 2 well-greased 7½×4×2¾-inch loaf pans and bake in a 350° oven for 25 minutes or until a toothpick comes out clean. Drizzle with Powdered Sugar Frosting and sprinkle with red sugar.

Powdered Sugar Frosting

- 2 cups sifted powdered sugar
- 2 tablespoons milk
- 1 tablespoon melted butter

In a bowl, beat all ingredients together until creamy and well blended.

Egg Casserole

This breakfast treat is sure to become a favorite Christmas morning tradition.

WHAT YOU NEED

- 12 eggs
- 2 cups milk
- 2 12-ounce packages frozen waffles (14 waffles)
- 8 ounces shredded cheddar cheese
- 1 cup cubed ham

WHAT YOU DO

Break eggs into large bowl and beat until blended. Add milk. Mix together. Layer ingredients in an 8-inch square baking dish starting with waffles and then adding the ham and cheese. Pour half of the egg/milk mixture over first layer. Continue layering ingredients, ending with cheese. Pour remaining egg/milk mixture over final layer. Refrigerate overnight. Remove from refrigerator. Bake in a 325° oven for 1 hour and 15 minutes. Serve hot. Makes 9 servings.

These surprisingly easy-to-make Scottish treats make a cup of coffee or a pot of tea even more inviting.

Merry Cherry Scones

WHAT YOU NEED

2½ cups flour

5 tablespoons sugar

2 teaspoons baking powder

¼ teaspoon salt

½ cup coconut

½ cup butter

½ cup dried cherries

2 tablespoons grated orange rind

½ cup milk

2 eggs

3 tablespoons milk

Coarse red sugar

WHAT YOU DO

In a large bowl, mix together dry ingredients and coconut; cut in butter. Stir in cherries and orange peel. In a separate bowl, mix together ½ cup milk and eggs. Make a well in the dry ingredients. Add milk and egg mixture. Stir until just moistened. Turn dough onto floured surface. Knead 7 to 9 times (dough will be sticky). On a lightly greased baking sheet, pat dough into an 8-inch circle. Cut into 10 wedges but do not separate. Brush with 3 tablespoons milk and sprinkle with red sugar. Bake in a 400° oven for 20 minutes. Place on a wire rack. Separate scones; store in an airtight container. Makes 10 scones.

Heart-Healthy Muffins

Please your palate and your body, too, with these tasty and good-for-you hearty oatmeal muffins.

WHAT YOU NEED

2¼ cups flour

2 cups oatmeal

⅔ cup sugar

2 teaspoons baking powder

½ teaspoon soda

¼ teaspoon salt

⅓ cup dried cranberries

⅓ cup canola oil

1 whole egg plus 1 egg white

1 cup buttermilk

¾ cup favorite jam

Oatmeal Topping

3 tablespoons sugar

1 teaspoon cinnamon

3 tablespoons oatmeal

2 tablespoons canola oil

WHAT YOU DO

In a large bowl, mix dry ingredients and dried cranberries. In a small bowl, whip oil, eggs, and buttermilk. Make a well in dry ingredients and add oil mixture. Mix until just combined. Do not overmix. Spoon into greased muffin cups, filling about ¾ full. Make an indentation in the center of each muffin and add 1 tablespoon of jam. Mix all ingredients for Oatmeal Topping and sprinkle on tops of muffins. Bake in a 400° oven for 15 minutes or until lightly browned. Makes 12 muffins.

Fresh Corn Chowder

Perfect for cold winter nights, this fresh corn chowder warms heart and soul with its creamy milk base and colorful vegetables.

WHAT YOU NEED

- 2 tablespoons butter
- 1 small onion, chopped
- ¼ cup diced carrots
- ¼ cup chopped celery
- ¼ cup chopped red and green peppers
- 2 tablespoons flour
- 1 teaspoon salt
- 1 teaspoon pepper
- 1 14 oz.-can chicken broth
- 1 cup fresh or frozen corn
- ¾ cup cream
- 1 cup milk

WHAT YOU DO

Melt butter in heavy saucepan. Saute onion, carrots, celery, and red and green peppers in the butter. Set aside. Mix flour, salt, pepper and chicken broth together. Add to vegetables and bring to a boil. If using fresh corn, cook on the cob and drain. Slice off the cob. Add fresh or frozen corn, cream, and milk to soup mixture. Heat thoroughly without boiling. Simmer until ready to serve. Makes about 6 servings.

Like the shining ribbons on your pretty Christmas packages, this beautiful salad is sure to be the children's favorite year after year.

Ribbon Salad

 WHAT YOU NEED

- 1   *3-oz. package lime gelatin*
- 1   *3-oz. package lemon gelatin*
- 16   *tiny marshmallows*
- 1   *3-ounce package cream cheese*
- 1   *8-oz. can crushed pineapple, drained*
- 1   *cup water*
- 1   *envelope whipped topping mix (such as Dream Whip)*
- 1   *3-oz. package red strawberry gelatin*

 WHAT YOU DO

Mix the lime gelatin as directed on package and pour into an 8×8-inch glass cake pan. Chill until firm. Mix the lemon gelatin with 1 cup boiling water. Add marshmallows and cream cheese until melted. Add crushed pineapple, 1 cup water, and the prepared whipped cream mix. Pour on top of the set green gelatin. Allow second layer to set approximately 1 hour. Mix red gelatin according to package directions. Let cool until syrupy; pour over the lemon gelatin layer. Allow to set until firm before serving. Garnish with sliced strawberry and fresh pineapple wedge if desired. Makes 12 servings.

MAKE IT TOGETHER

IT IS FUN AND ALMOST MAGICAL TO MAKE GELATIN. LET THE CHILDREN HELP MIX THE GELATIN POWDER INTO THE WATER AND SEE THE GLORIOUS COLORS. MAKE IT A FAMILY TRADITION TO MAKE THIS SALAD TOGETHER EVERY YEAR.

Christmas Eve Chili

Come in from the cold and warm up with some piping hot chili. Serve with cheese and crackers or wheat rolls and honey butter.

WHAT YOU NEED

- 1 small onion, chopped
- 1 small red pepper, chopped
- 1 small green pepper, chopped
- 2 tablespoons olive oil
- 2 lbs. lean ground beef
- 2 14.5-oz cans diced tomatoes
- 1 14.5-oz. can whole tomatoes
- 1 28-oz. can crushed tomatoes
- 1 14.5-oz. can chili beans
- 2 teaspoons chili powder
- 1 teaspoon minced garlic
- 1 teaspoon black pepper
- ½ teaspoon salt
  Star pasta and sliced cheese (optional)

WHAT YOU DO

In a large saucepan, saute onions and peppers in the olive oil. Add ground beef and cook thoroughly. Drain well. Add tomatoes, beans, and seasonings. Cook until bubbly. Continue cooking on low heat, stirring often for 30 minutes. *If cooking in a crock pot,* transfer cooked onion, peppers, and ground beef to crock pot. Add all other ingredients. Cook on high heat for 4 to 5 hours. Makes about 8 large servings. Garnish with star pasta and slices of cheese if desired.

Candies and Sweet Treats

Red and white swirl happily together to make this pretty Christmas candy a work of art.

WHAT YOU NEED

3   cups sugar

1   12-ounce can evaporated milk

1   cup butter

2   7-ounce jars marshmallow creme

2   6-ounce packages white chocolate chips
Red paste food coloring
Peppermint candy canes, crushed (about four canes)

WHAT YOU DO

In heavy saucepan, combine sugar, evaporated milk, and butter. Boil for about 12 minutes or to soft ball stage (238° on a candy thermometer.) Remove from heat. Add the marshmallow creme and white chocolate chips, stirring until melted. Add food coloring, stirring to swirl. Pour into a greased, foil-lined 9x13-inch pan. Sprinkle with crushed candy canes; chill until set. Remove foil and candy from pan and cut into squares.

Peppermint Marble Fudge

Christmas Candied Apples

All covered in frosting and candy,
these sweet apples are good enough to
dream about. Make plenty to give as
gifts to good girls and boys.

 WHAT YOU NEED

½ *package caramels*
  (about ½ pound)

2 to 3 *tablespoons milk*

  Apples; wooden apple sticks

  Red food coloring

  White chocolate

  Green gumdrops; sugar

  Cinnamon red hots

  Peppermint sticks

  Sprinkles

MAKE IT A GIFT

TIE A RIBBON ON THE
STICK (AND CELLOPHANE
AROUND THE APPLE, IF
DESIRED) AND PRESENT
AS A GIFT.

 WHAT YOU DO

In a microwave, melt the
caramels and milk, stirring
frequently. Insert sticks
into the apples and dip
into the melted caramel
mixture. (We soaked our
sticks in red food coloring
to color them slightly.)
Let caramel excess drip
off. If desired, dip bottoms
in white sprinkles. Place
apples on a piece of
greased foil. In a small
bowl, melt the white
chocolate on 50%
microwave power. Transfer
to a disposable decorating
bag. Snip the tip of the
bag; drizzle the melted
chocolate over the apples.
If desired, while chocolate
is still wet sprinkle with
crushed peppermint sticks.
For holly, roll out green
gumdrops in a generous
amount of granulated
sugar. Cut with a small
leaf-shaped cookie cutter.
Use red hots for holly
berries. Arrange the leaves
in the wet chocolate
drizzle. Let the white
chocolate set before
wrapping. Chill to store.

Try your hand at making jelly or jam this
year. Combine this sweet treat with a hearty
loaf of bread for a great holiday gift.

Sweet Jam and Jelly

WHAT YOU NEED

For the Pinecot Jam

5½ cups fruit (1 can crushed
    pineapple in juice,
    2¾ lbs. fresh apricots,
    pitted and diced)

1 1¾-oz. package powdered
    fruit pectin

½ teaspoon butter

6 cups sugar

For the Cran-Strawberry or Green Apple Jelly

4 cups cran-strawberry juice
    or apple juice colored
    with green food coloring

¼ cup lemon juice

1 1¾-oz. package powdered
    fruit pectin

4½ cups sugar

MAKE IT A GIFT

CUT OUT A CIRCLE OF COLORED
PAPER TO FIT THE JAR TOP. DECORATE
THE PAPER WITH A GOLD PEN.
PLACE ON TOP OF THE JAR FLAT.
TIE ALL THE JARS TOGETHER WITH
A GOLD RIBBON.

WHAT YOU DO

For the Pinecot Jam

(shown at far left) In a Dutch oven or kettle, combine fruit and pectin. Bring to boil. Boil over high heat, stirring constantly. Stir in sugar all at once. Bring to a full rolling boil; boil hard 1 minute stirring constantly. Remove from heat. Quickly skim off foam with a metal spoon. Immediately ladle jam into hot, sterilized pint canning jars, leaving ¼-inch headspace. Wipe jar rims and adjust lids. Process in a boiling-water canner for 5 minutes. Remove jars. Cool on racks. Makes 4 pints.

For the jellies *(shown in stacked jars)*

In a Dutch oven or kettle, combine fruit juice, lemon juice, and pectin. Bring to boil. Boil over high heat stirring constantly. Stir in sugar all at once. Bring to a full rolling boil; boil hard 1 minute stirring constantly. Remove from heat. Quickly skim off foam with a metal spoon. Immediately ladle jelly into hot, sterilized half-pint canning jars, leaving ¼-inch headspace. Wipe jar rims and adjust lids. Process in a boiling-water canner for 5 minutes. Remove jars. Cool on racks. Makes 6 half-pints.

Cashew Coconut Brittle

WHAT YOU NEED

2 cups sugar

1 cup light corn syrup

½ cup water

½ teaspoon salt

2 tablespoons butter

2 cups cashews

2 teaspoons baking soda

1 teaspoon vanilla

1 cup freshly shredded
coconut

WHAT YOU DO

In a heavy 4-quart saucepan, heat sugar, syrup, water, and salt. Bring mixture to a boil; add butter. Using a candy thermometer, stir frequently until mixture reaches 250°. Add cashews, stirring constantly, until thermometer reaches 305°. Remove from heat and quickly stir in baking soda and vanilla. Mix well; add coconut. Continue to mix well. Pour into 2 warm, well-buttered baking sheets. Spread into thin sheets. Let cool. Break into bite-size pieces.

MAKE IT A GIFT
DECORATE TINY PURCHASED VELLUM ENVELOPES AND FILL WITH ONE OR TWO PIECES OF THIS SWEET TREAT.

Crunchy, sweet, and with an
unexpected heavenly taste combination
of cashews and coconut, this candy
is hard to resist.

Sugar-Sweet Popcorn Mix

All dressed up in a pretty red sugar coating, this simple mix is sure to please every sweet tooth.

WHAT YOU NEED

20 *cups popped popcorn*

2 *cups sugar*

1 *cup butter*

½ *cup light corn syrup*

½ *teaspoon salt*

Food coloring

1 *tablespoon clear vanilla*

½ *teaspoon baking soda*

Red and green gumdrops

WHAT YOU DO

Pop the popcorn and remove all hulls and unpopped kernels. Spread the popcorn in a large greased cake pan. Set aside. Bring the sugar, butter, corn syrup, salt, and food coloring to a boil and boil for five minutes. Remove from heat and add vanilla and baking soda. Immediately pour over popped popcorn. Stir until popcorn is covered. Bake in 250° degree oven for 1 hour, stirring every 15 minutes. Remove from oven and let cool. Cut up red and green gumdrops and toss with popcorn.

MAKE IT A GIFT

EVERYONE ON YOUR CHRISTMAS LIST WOULD LOVE A BAG OF THIS YUMMY SWEET TREAT. ADHERE TINY DOT STICKERS TO A SMALL CELLOPHANE BAG AND TIE WITH SILVER CORDING TO MAKE PERSONALIZED GIFT BAGS OF POPCORN.

Homemade Marshmallows

Who would imagine that this sweet and soft treat is so easy to make? Tint your marshmallows with the colors of the season.

WHAT YOU NEED

- 2 tablespoons *unflavored gelatin*
- ¼ cup *cold water*
- 1 teaspoon *clear vanilla*
- ½ teaspoon *salt*
- 2 cups *sugar*
- ¾ cup *boiling water*
- *Powdered sugar*

WHAT YOU DO

Butter an 8x8-inch square glass cake pan. Set aside. Put cold water into small measuring cup. Sprinkle gelatin into water to dissolve. Pour into mixing bowl and add vanilla and salt. Set aside. Boil sugar and water to soft ball stage (238°). Pour syrup slowly over the gelatin, mixing on high speed, until mixture turns very thick and white. Color with food coloring if desired. Pour into a buttered pan. Dust with powdered sugar. Let stand overnight. Cut into small squares. After cutting, dust with powdered sugar again if desired.

Candied Citrus Peel

Full of flavor and fragrance, this treat can be used in cakes and breads or enjoyed as a candy all by itself.

WHAT YOU NEED

- 2 oranges or 2 lemons
- 6 cups water
- 2 cups sugar
- 1 cup water
- 1 cup sugar

WHAT YOU DO

Cut the oranges or lemons in half and squeeze out juice. Boil the rinds in 6 cups of water for 30 minutes. Drain. With a spoon carefully scrape out all the white pith, leaving just the outside peel. Cut the peel into strips with scissors. Mix 2 cups sugar with 1 cup water and bring to boiling. Add cut peel and simmer for 45 minutes, stirring occasionally. Drain using a sieve. Toss drained peel in 1 cup sugar to coat. Lay out on a single layer of waxed paper to dry overnight. Store in a closed container.

MAKE IT A GIFT

CUT A SMALL ORANGE IN HALF AND SCOOP OUT THE INSIDE. MAKE A TINY CUT EVERY INCH AROUND THE TOP OF THE HALF ORANGE. THREAD A TINY RIBBON IN AND OUT OF THE CUTS. TIE WITH A BOW. FILL WITH CANDIED CITRUS PEEL.

More Ideas
for holiday goodies

 Make a place card for everyone at the table using a fresh pear. Write the name of each guest on a small piece of gold cardstock. Make a tiny slit in the pear and put the name tag in the slit. Tie a bow around the stem of the pear. Set the pear just above the plate on the table.

 Purchase small inexpensive holiday plates and large fabric Christmas napkins at discount stores. Arrange your favorite cookies or candies on the plates. Set the plate in the center of the napkin, bring the four corners together and tie with a ribbon.

 If frosting and decorating cookies seems too big a task this year, cut out the shapes with a cookie cutter and brush with milk before baking. Add a sprinkle of colored sugar and the cookies will have a lovely color after baking.

 Simple holiday garnishes make any recipe seem like a Christmas recipe. Try using colored or holiday-shaped pastas in casseroles or pasta salads. Use red and green holiday-shaped gumdrops to decorate a favorite cake, and red sugar on top of whipped toppings.

 Purchase an inexpensive white fabric tablecloth. Let the children draw their favorite Christmas cookies and other holiday foods on the cloth with permanent markers or paint pens. Use the tablecloth at the children's table for the holiday meal.

 For a special Christmas morning breakfast, make pancakes in the shape of bells, Christmas trees, and stars. This simple idea will bring a smile to everyone's face and will set the tone for a wonderful Christmas day.

"The stockings were hung by the chimney with care."

—A VISIT FROM ST. NICHOLAS (1823)

make the
season
bright
with
festive
decorating
ideas

They may just look like pretty packages,
but these presents serve a purpose. Make
a set for your holiday decorating and make
an extra set for a special book-lovers gift.

Package Bookends

WHAT YOU NEED

Small gift boxes

Tiny rocks or fish gravel

Transparent tape

Wrapping paper and ribbon to
  match vintage books

Purchased bottlebrush tree

Tacky crafts glue

WHAT YOU DO

Fill each of the packages
with the tiny rocks or fish
gravel. Tape the boxes
closed. Wrap the packages
with wrapping paper and
ribbons to coordinate with
the books to be used. (We
used red and green vintage
books.) Stack and glue the
boxes together forming
the book ends. Glue a
small bottlebrush tree to
the top of the box if
desired. Place the pieces on
either side of the books
forming the bookends.

What could be easier than hanging a fresh basket of fruit at your front door to greet your holiday guests.

Fruit Basket Welcome

WHAT YOU NEED

Wicker basket with one flat side (available at crafts and discount stores)
Fresh fruit and nuts
Fresh greens
Red ribbon

WHAT YOU DO

Weave the ribbon through the wicker basket and tie a bow in the front. Hang the basket on the inside of an outdoor walkway or doorway being sure that the nails or hanger will accommodate heavy fruits. Fill the basket with greens, a variety of fruits, and nuts. In cool climates the basket of fruit will keep for a week or more.

MAKE IT TONIGHT

THIS WELCOMING TRIM TAKES ONLY MOMENTS TO MAKE AND CREATES A GRAND STATEMENT.

Topper Collection

Trace the full-size patterns on *pages 130–131* and cut out.

WHAT YOU DO

Trace the full-size patterns on *pages 130–131* and cut out. Trace around star patterns onto wood; cut out with a band saw. Drill a hole in the center of each star. Glue dowel into the hole. Let dry. Paint the entire piece with silver paint. Let dry. Trim with gold glitter as indicated by the lines on the pattern. Dowel length can be adjusted to fit different styles and heights of tree toppers.

WHAT YOU NEED

Tracing paper; pencil; scissors

2-foot length of ½-inch pine

Band saw

¼-inch drill and bit

¼-inch dowel cut into 4- or 5-inch lengths

Silver craft paint; paintbrush

Tacky crafts glue

Fine gold glitter

Vintage tree toppers are favorite holiday collectibles but are difficult to display. Here is an idea that turns your favorite toppers into an elegant holiday centerpiece.

129

Tree Topper Collection continued

ASYMETRICAL STAR

FOUR-POINTED STAR

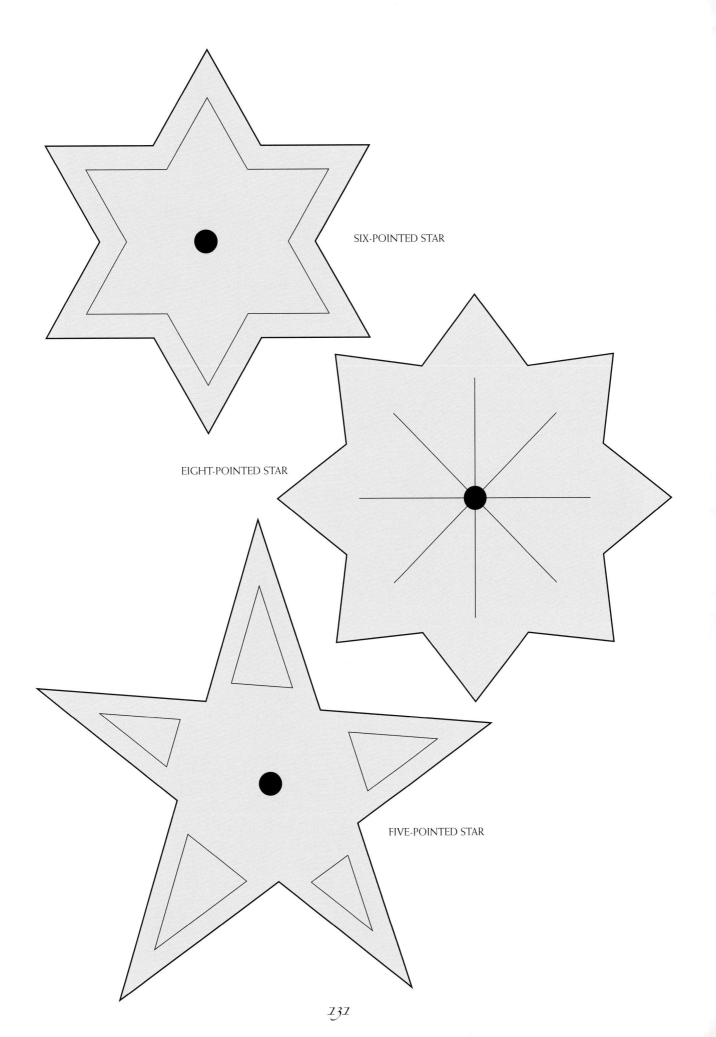

SIX-POINTED STAR

EIGHT-POINTED STAR

FIVE-POINTED STAR

Pretty Paper Houses

WHAT YOU NEED

Tracing paper

Pencil

Cardstock papers in pastel colors and white

Scissors

Crafts knife

Tacky crafts glue

Small (2½-inch) bottlebrush trees (available at crafts stores)

Scrap of yellow cellophane

Fine glitter to match house color

Fine white glitter

MAKE IT TOGETHER

WHAT FUN TO BUILD THESE HOUSES TOGETHER. LET THE CHILDREN HELP FOLD AFTER YOU SCORE THE LINES. LET EVERYONE SPRINKLE THE GLITTER ON THESE MAGICAL HOUSES.

WHAT YOU DO

Trace the house patterns, pages 134-135, onto tracing paper, marking all tab and fold lines. Cut out. In addition to these patterns, cut a 5×3¼-inch rectangle on white cardstock for each house base. Draw a 1¾×4¾-inch rectangle on light pink cardstock for the pink house roof. Score and fold this roof in half. Draw the blue house roof pattern onto white. Draw all of the other house pieces on colored cardstock. Cut out the patterns. Cut out the window and door openings using a crafts knife. Cut a piece of cellophane ¼-inch bigger than window openings. Glue cellophane inside the window openings. Score and fold the tabs on all of the house patterns. *For the pink house,* cut a slit in the house front. Fold and score the overhang in half and attach. Assemble houses by gluing folded tabs together. Attach the house sides to the house back; glue to base. Glue a tree inside the house. Attach the roofs. Glue doors to door openings. Add a chimney if desired. Glue a tree to the base. Use crafts glue to make a line around the windows. Sprinkle with fine glitter to match house color. Using glue, add white glitter to house roofs, chimneys and edges.

Recreate the sweet paper houses so
popular at holiday time in the mid-20th
century by using today's cardstock papers
in soft colors. A sprinkle of glitter brings
the houses a blanket of glistening snow.

Pretty Paper Houses continued

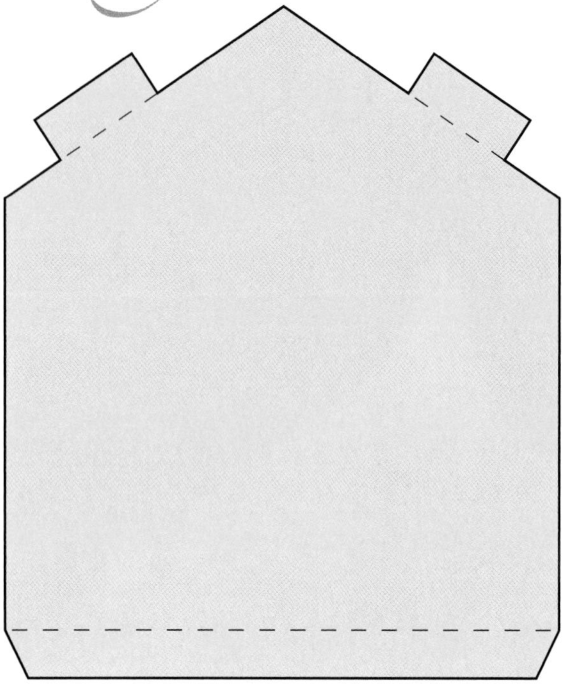

PINK HOUSE BACK

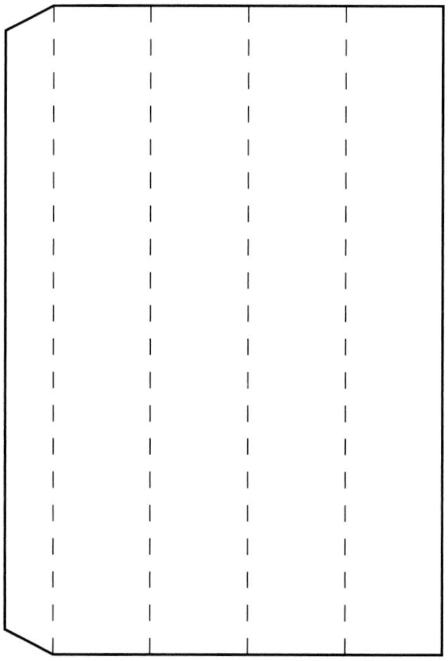

PINK OR BLUE HOUSE CHIMNEY (OPTIONAL)

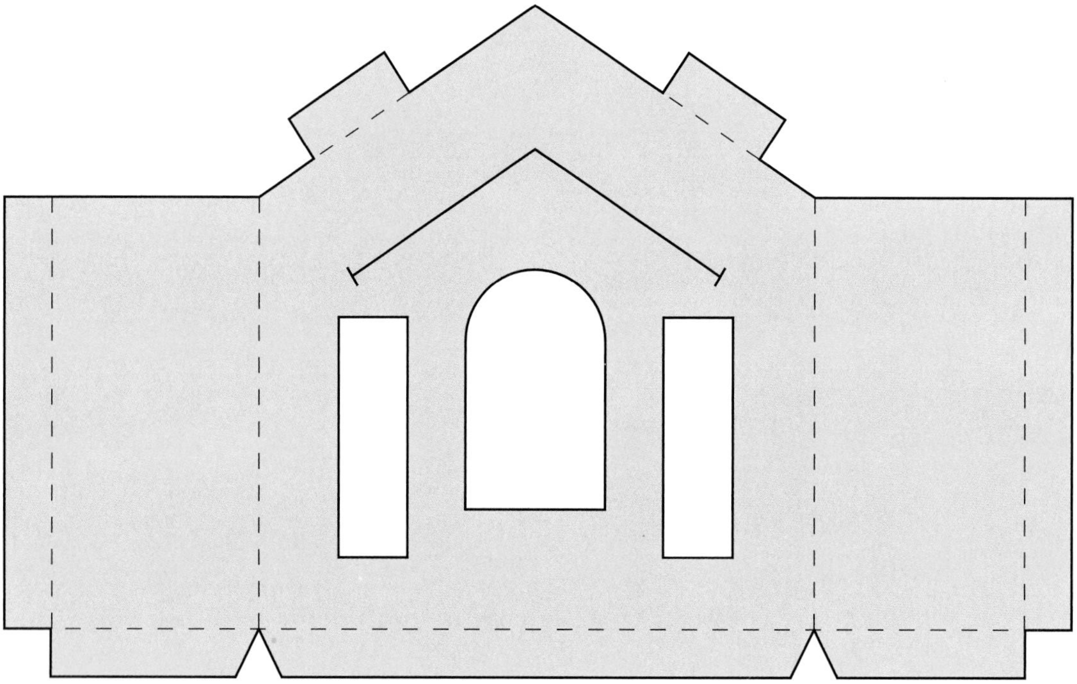

PINK HOUSE FRONT

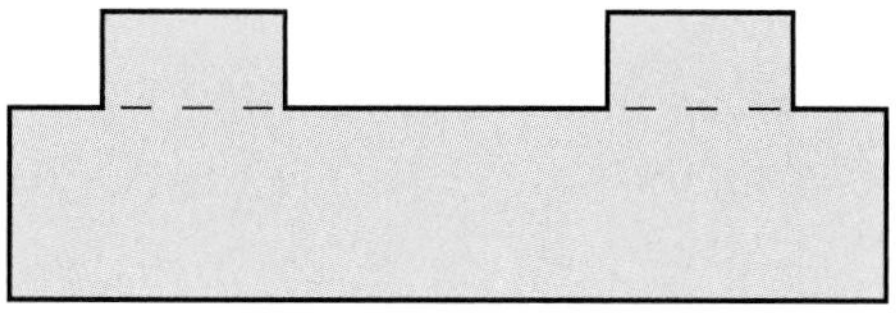

PINK HOUSE OVERHANG

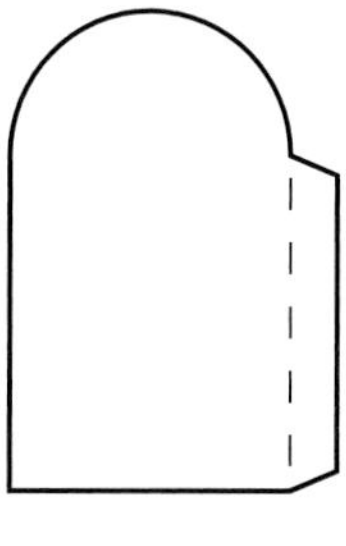

PINK HOUSE DOOR

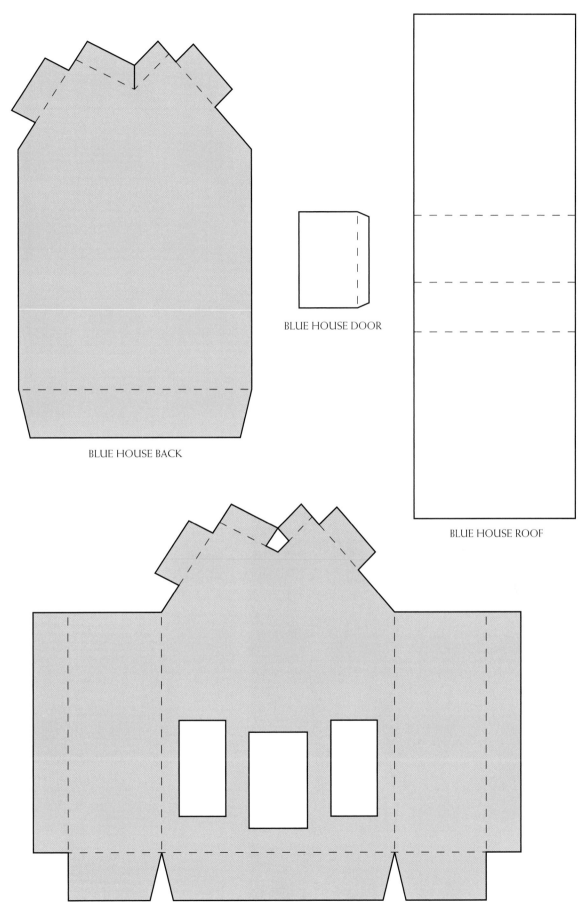

BLUE HOUSE BACK

BLUE HOUSE DOOR

BLUE HOUSE ROOF

BLUE HOUSE FRONT AND SIDES

Your guests will never lose track of their party glasses when wearing special charms designed just for them.

Charming Goblet Jewelry

MAKE IT A GIFT

THESE CLEVER PIECES OF GOBLET JEWELRY ARE A SNAP TO MAKE. MAKE A SET FOR YOURSELF AND ONE FOR YOUR FRIENDS. GIVE THE CHARMING JEWELRY AWAY WITH A SET OF FOUR CRYSTAL GOBLETS FOR A SPECTACULAR GIFT.

WHAT YOU NEED

Gold metallic chenille stems
Scissors
Small colorful beads with holes just big enough to fit over chenille stems
Charms or small ornaments

WHAT YOU DO

Cut chenille stems to measure four inches. String the beads onto the chenille stems, adding a charm or small ornament in the center. Form a hook at the end of each chenille stem. Wrap the jewelry around the base of the goblet and hook the two ends together.

Pine Cone Santas

WHAT YOU NEED

Medium-size pine cone

White acrylic paint; paintbrush

Small Santa head ornament

Strong crafts glue (such as E6000)

White air-dry clay (such as Model Magic)

Purchased small package

Small bottlebrush tree

Fine white glitter

These friendly Santas will bring smiles to everyone who sees them. Let each jolly soul carry a unique holiday trim.

WHAT YOU DO

Choose pine cones with flat bottoms and a flat top. Pull off fronds if necessary to flatten. Paint the edges of the pine cone with white paint. Set aside to dry. Form arms and feet for the Santa using the air dry clay. Make arms by rolling a piece of clay about the size of a marble into a log shape and pointing one end. Curve the arms and poke into the pine cone to dry. Make feet by rolling two balls of clay about the size of a marble. Elongate the clay and push into the bottom of the pine cone to dry, flattening the bottom of the feet to level the pine cone body. After the clay has dried overnight, gently remove it from the pine cone and glue it back in place. Glue the ornament head to the top of the pine cone. Glue a package or tree to one arm. Dust arms and feet with glue and fine white glitter. Let dry.

These Christmas stockings have a secret of their own—they were each made from fabrics that had served a practical purpose before they were transformed into such elegant holiday pieces.

Vintage Stockings

WHAT YOU NEED

Tracing paper; pencil; scissors
Fabric in desired colors
  (we used 1930s feedsack-print
  fabrics, 1960s vintage drapery
  fabric, and velveteen from a
  castaway 1950s skirt)
¼ yard iron-on fleece
¼ yard lining fabric
⅛ yard desired fabric for cuff
¼-inch solid color piping
  (for small stocking only)
Fusible webbing; white glitter
  paint in a tube (for red
  stocking only)
Threads to match fabrics

WHAT YOU DO

For the Small Country Stockings (*at left*), enlarge and trace the patterns on *page 140* onto tracing paper. Cut out the patterns. With right sides of stocking fabric together, cut two stocking shapes adding ¼-inch seam allowances on all sides and ½-inch seam allowance at the top. Cut two pieces of iron-on fleece the same size. Cut two lining pieces without adding ¼-inch seam allowances. For loop,

SMALL COUNTRY STOCKINGS

GOLDEN
STOCKING

cut a 2×6-inch piece of
fabric. Iron fleece to the
wrong side of each
stocking. Baste piping to
edge of stocking front.

Sew stocking pieces
together, right sides
together being careful not
to catch piping in the seam.
Clip curves; turn right side

out. Press. Stitch lining
together with right sides
together using a ¼-inch

continued on page 140

139

seam. Clip curves. Turn; insert lining inside stocking. Baste across top of lining and stocking ½ inch from stocking top. *For loop,* fold long edges of fabric into the middle and over in half again to make a ½×6-inch piece. Stitch close to fold. Fold in half with top raw edges even. Place loop inside lining of stocking and baste to top edge of stocking. *For small stocking cuff,* fold cuff fabric in half right sides together; place cuff pattern on fold as indicated on pattern. Cut out 2 cuff pieces leaving ¼-inch seam allowances at cuff sides and ½-inch seam allowance at top. From pattern, cut one fleece cuff piece without adding seam allowances. Cut along fold line making two pieces. Iron fleece to back of each cuff fabric, covering only half of each cuff. Machine or hand quilt the cuff, if desired. Open up cuff and with right sides together, stitch the sides of the cuff

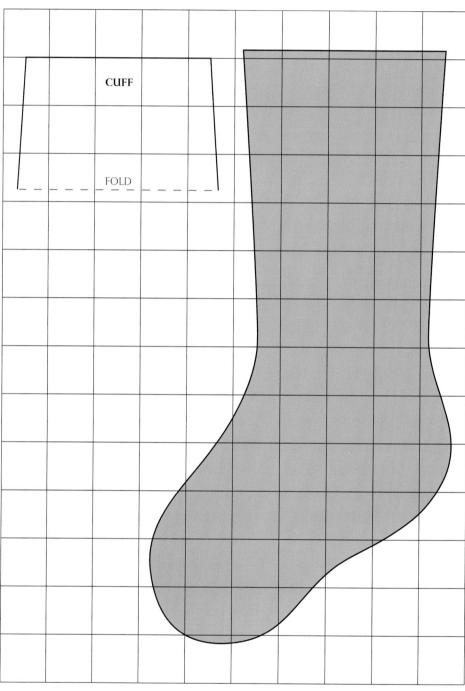

SMALL COUNTRY STOCKING PATTERNS

1 SQUARE = 1 INCH
ENLARGE AT 200%

with ¼-inch seams. Fold cuff in half to form a ring. Put cuff inside stocking, with top raw edges even

and right side of cuff facing lining. Stitch top together with ½-inch seam. Flip cuff to outside

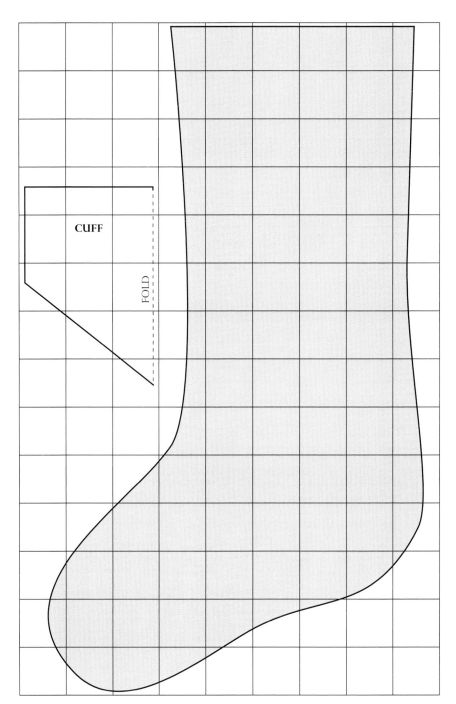

CUFF

FOLD

LARGE GOLDEN OR RED POLKA-DOT STOCKING PATTERNS

1 SQUARE = 1 INCH
ENLARGE AT 200 %

**RED
POLKA DOT
STOCKING**

over stocking. Press. **For Golden Stocking** *page 139,* and **Red Polka Dot Stocking,** *above,* cut large stocking pieces as for small stocking except for cuff. *To make polka-dots on red stocking,* cut ⅝-inch, 1-inch, and 1½-inch

circles from cuff fabric. Fuse to front of stocking using fusible webbing. Use glitter paint pen to draw around dots. Let dry. Stitch as for small stocking omitting piping. *For cuffs,* cut 4 cuff pieces from cuff pattern placing pattern on

fold as indicated on pattern. Cut 2 fleece cuff patterns without adding seam allowances. Open up cuffs. Iron fleece to wrong side of two cuff pieces. With right sides together, stitch bottom pointed edges using ¼-inch seams. Turn and press flat. Quilt as desired. Join cuffs together at side seams, right sides together, using a ¼-inch seam. Baste loop to top edge of stocking; insert cuff into stocking, with right side of cuff facing lining and raw edges at top even. Sew, with ½-inch seam, around top edge, through cuff, stocking, and loop. Clip edges. Turn cuff to outside, rolling over top edge of stocking to complete. Press.

Christmas Lights Under Glass

Collect those wonderful lights from years gone by and display them for all to see.

WHAT YOU NEED
Glass jars or other glass containers with lids
Antique or vintage Christmas lights and bulbs such as bubble lights, lights on cording, and Santa light bulbs

WHAT YOU DO
Organize the lights by color, shape, or age. Wash and dry the glass jars. Try different combinations of the lights in various jars. Arrange with holly and greens on a glass tray.

MAKE IT TOGETHER
LET THE LITTLE ONES HELP BY GROUPING THE LIGHT BULBS BY COLOR. CHOOSE LIGHTS FROM EACH OF THEIR COLOR GROUPINGS TO MAKE THE ARRANGEMENT.

Sparkling Holiday Frames

WHAT YOU DO

Arrange stickers on the frames as desired. Try to choose sticker sheets that have some line stickers included that connect the individual stickers. This makes for a more cohesive design. After the stickers are all in place, use your finger to rub some clear glue very lightly over the stickers and the frame. Dust lightly with the fine glitter. Allow to dry. Using old photos, prints, or copies of the antique postcards on *page 188*, put pictures in the frames.

WHAT YOU NEED

Purchased wooden picture frames (ours have a 4×6-inch opening that accommodates the antique postcards shown)

Purchased holiday stickers

Clear crafts glue (such as Suze Gluez)

Fine white glitter

MAKE IT A GIFT

CHOOSE PICTURES OF YOU AND YOUR FRIENDS OR FAMILY MEMBERS AND FRAME THEM IN THESE SPARKLING FRAMES. THE GIFT WILL MEAN EVEN MORE WITH A PICTURE OF YOU TOGETHER IN IT.

Purchased wooden picture frames are
dressed for the holidays with Christmas
stickers and ultra-fine glitter.

Beautiful Birdie Globes

Catching the light of the winter sun, these glistening balls of ice are filled with goodies for your favorite feathered friends.

WHAT YOU NEED

Round balloons

Bird seed; orange peel

Dried cranberries or other
dried fruits; funnel (optional)

Water; freezer

WHAT YOU DO

Drop the bird seed, dried fruit, and orange peel into the empty balloon. (Use a funnel if necessary.) Fill the balloon with water and tie a knot at the top. Place in the freezer turning the balloon every 20 minutes until frozen. Remove from freezer and peel off balloon. Set outside in cold weather for the birds.

MAKE IT TOGETHER

GIVE EACH FAMILY MEMBER A JOB IN MAKING THESE FUN PROJECTS. LET ONE CHILD FILL THE BALLOONS WITH SEEDS AND ONE CHILD BE IN CHARGE OF TURNING THE BALLOONS IN THE FREEZER. IT WILL BE EVERYONE'S JOB TO WATCH THE HAPPY BIRDS.

Noah's Ark Animals

Shimmering with sparkling glitter, these animals will decorate any corner of your house—two by two.

WHAT YOU NEED

Newspapers

Purchased plastic-toy zoo
animals (two of each species),
large size for decorations;
small size for ornaments

Primer paint (such as Kilz)

Spray paint in metallic colors

Acrylic paint in desired colors

Paintbrushes; crafts glue

Fine glitter in desired colors

Drill and ⅛-inch drill bit

Narrow ribbon; paper punch

WHAT YOU DO

Cover the work area with newspapers. Spray all of the toys with primer. Allow to dry. Spray-paint the desired color of metallic paint, turning the toys as necessary. We used gold, copper, platinum, and silver. Use two coats if necessary. Allow to dry thoroughly. Paint eyes, dots, lines, ears, and other

continued on page 150

148

Noah's Ark Animals continued

desired areas with acrylic paint and dust with glitter of the same color. Follow the lines in the molded plastic of the animals as a guide. Use glue when necessary to add more glitter to other areas. Refer to the photos on *pages 148–152* for ideas. Let all paint and glue dry thoroughly. *For the hanging ornament animals,* drill a hole in the front upper portion of the small-size animal toys. Paint as for the larger animals. Allow to dry and put a ribbon through the hole to hang.

continued on page 152

Noah's Ark Animals continued

To make the coordinating hanging *Noah's Ark ornament,* photocopy the image on *page 189* onto cardstock. Cut out the image. Curve the edges slightly; punch a hole in the corner. Put a ribbon in the hole for hanging.

More Ideas
for festive decorating

Use purchased garlands of beads to tie back drapes or curtains. Most beaded garlands can be cut anywhere on the string. Cut a section approximately 24 inches long and loop around the drape or curtain tying a knot in the front. Let the tails hang down in front of the fabric.

Set a wicker basket of tiny wrapped gifts nestled in fresh greens inside your front door. As each guest arrives, have them choose a gift to keep as their memory of your holiday gathering.

Attach rope lights designed for outdoor lighting around the edge of a vintage sled following the shape of the piece. When the lights are on, the sled will light up as a beautiful silhouette.

Add fresh greens or holly to unexpected places in your home.

Tuck them under centerpieces, on windowsills, around picture frames, and on top of cupboards to add a festive holiday touch.

For your banister this year, use a fruit theme. Attach fresh or artificial greens to the banister and then wire oranges, limes, and lemons into the greens. Add curls of orange, lime, and lemon rind to finish the look and to add a fruity aroma.

Purchase monogram letters that spell the words, "Noel" or "Joy." Glue each monogram letter to a piece of colored felt and frame each one in a small gold or silver frame. Arrange the frames to spell the word and place on the mantel or buffet for all to enjoy.

Sew a wide holiday-colored ribbon on an inexpensive purchased pillow for a quick and simple decorating idea.

"Christmas won't be Christmas without any presents."

—LITTLE WOMEN (1868)

put a *twinkle* in their eyes with **gifts** and **wraps** you make

Inexpensive dominoes take on a new role as clever coasters, perfect for that game–playing friend of yours.

Polka Dot Coasters

MAKE IT TOGETHER

BUY TWO BOXES OF DOMINOES AND GATHER GRANDMA, GRANDPA, AND THE KIDS TOGETHER FOR A GAME WHILE YOU ALL MAKE THESE SIMPLE COASTERS.

WHAT YOU NEED

1½-inch wooden dominoes
Small sheet of cork backing
¼-inch-wide metallic red braiding
Strong crafts glue (such as E6000)

WHAT YOU DO

Cut cork backing to measure 3¼×3¼ inches. Arrange dominoes as desired on cork square. Glue to cork backing. Finish the edge by gluing the braiding around the coaster edge.

To wrap, place in box; tie with polka dot ribbon. **For tag,** cut rectangles from black and red paper referring to photo, *above.* Punch holes in red paper to resemble domino. Glue to black paper; add name with metallic marker.

Jingle Bell Soap

The colors of Christmas shimmer through these festive bars of handmade glycerin soap.

WHAT YOU NEED

Green glycerin soap block

Green coconut oil soap block

Knife

Glass measuring cup

Small red jingle bells

Purchased plastic soap molds

WHAT YOU DO

Cut the green glycerin soap into small pieces; place into measuring cup. Set aside. Carefully slice ½-inch thick pieces of the green coconut oil soap. Cut the slices into holly shapes.

Arrange holly shapes in the plastic soap molds adding red jingle bells for the berries. Melt glycerin soap in microwave until just melted. Cool until a thin film appears over the top of the soap. Skim film aside and pour carefully into the molds. Allow to set. Remove soap from molds.

To wrap, use small florist cellophane bags (available at florist shops). Put the soap into bag; tie with cording and jingle bells.

**Simple glittered holiday motifs
are added to purchased gift bags
to make these fun-to-give gifts.**

Christmas Fun Bags

MAKE IT TONIGHT

DRAW AROUND THE SHAPES OVER AND OVER AND CUT THEM OUT AND DECORATE THEM ALL AT ONCE. ATTACHING THEM TO THE BAGS IS A SNAP. YOU CAN MAKE ALL YOUR WRAPS IN ONE EVENING.

WHAT YOU NEED

Tracing paper; pencil; scissors

Purchased gift bags

Crafts foam sheets (such as Fun Foam) in desired colors

Round adhesive spacers (such as Pop Dots) (available at crafts or scrapbooking stores)

Holiday stickers

Tacky crafts glue

Fine glitter

WHAT YOU DO

Trace patterns, *left* and *below*, onto tracing paper. Cut out. Trace around the shapes onto crafts foam. Cut out. Decorate with stickers and glitter. Attach the shapes to front of bags using adhesive spacers. These adhere to both pieces and makes the motif stand out from the bag. Fill with Christmas goodies.

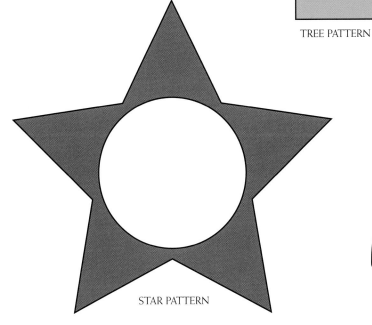

TREE PATTERN

STAR PATTERN

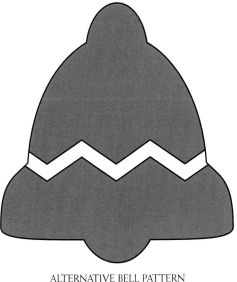

ALTERNATIVE BELL PATTERN

Everyone loves to wear beads! Here are some easy bracelet ideas for girls of all ages on your Christmas list.

Beaded *Bracelets*

WHAT YOU NEED

Beads in desired colors and styles
Gossamer elastic beading thread
Beading needle
Tacky crafts glue

Small unbreakable Christmas ornaments (for the green bracelet)
Charm or Christmas motif from old earrings or necklace (for red and green bracelet)

MAKE IT TOGETHER

HELP THE CHILDREN MAKE THESE EASY BEADED GIFTS FOR THEIR SPECIAL FRIENDS AND TEACHERS.

WHAT YOU DO

For the child's bracelet, string pink pearl beads and alphabet beads in desired order spelling the child's name. *For the green bracelet,* string a variety of green glass beads putting the unbreakable Christmas ornaments in the middle. *For the red and green bracelet,* string the beads and add a charm from an old holiday necklace or earring. *For all bracelets,* tie a double knot at the end and dot with glue.

Paper Stripes Wrap

Beautiful paper strips made for quilling come in all colors. Use these cut paper strips to embellish your holiday packages.

WHAT YOU NEED

*Package of quilling papers in
  desired colors*
Scissors
Buttons
Tacky crafts glue

WHAT YOU DO

Quilling papers come in various widths and in an array of colors. Choose the sizes and colors that match your wrapping paper. Glue the strips around the package securing in the back. To make the "bows" cut small strips of paper and curl with open scissors. Overlap and glue together leaving the paper ends all going up or securing some to stay underneath. Glue a button or stack of buttons in the center of the bow.

Personalized Containers of Goodies

People on your Christmas list like many different things. Here are some gifts to make that celebrate their favorite hobbies. You can be sure they'll be pleased with these personalized goodies.

THE NEEDLEWORK LOVER

A small sewing basket is the perfect holder for a collection of stitching items. Embroidery floss, needles, and fancy scissors are just a few of the things to put in this gift for a cross-stitcher.

THE FAIR PLAYER

Make good use of old playing cards by decoupaging them to the front of a purchased metal pail. Outline each one with glue and dust with red glitter. Fill with red tinsel garland, dice, poker chips, cards, and a rule book to keep it all above board.

THE HANDYMAN

Decorate a quart paint can and fill it with handy tools to have around the house. To make a clever wrap for the container, color-copy screws, nails, and other small toolbox items. Cut a strip from the color copy and glue it around the can. Glue a flat ribbon on both sides of the paper. Fill the can with a hammer, paintbrush, pliers, and other tools. Include a unique hammer cookie cutter to complete the gift.

THE GOOD COOK

Every good cook would love a sifter filled with great kitchen gadgets. There are so many to choose from in every color to match any kitchen. Fill the sifter with colored spatulas, a variety of whisks, wooden spoons, scissors, meat thermometer, and more. Tie a curly ribbon around the sifter and add a name tag embellished with silver star stickers.

Purchased yo-yos are even more fun with a little bright plastic paint and some shiny stickers.

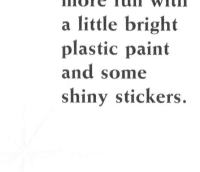

Painted Yo-Yos

WHAT YOU NEED

Purchased plastic yo-yo

Plastic paints in desired colors (available at crafts stores)

Paintbrushes

Shiny star stickers

Plastic bead

WHAT YOU DO

Cover the name brand of the yo-yo with a coat of plastic paint. Allow to dry. Add another coat of paint if needed. Let dry. Use contrasting colors of paint to add swirls and dots. Let dry. Use star stickers to decorate over the painted areas. Add a bead to the end of the string.

MAKE IT TOGETHER

THIS IS A FUN GIFT FOR CHILDREN TO MAKE FOR THEIR FRIENDS. LET EACH ARTIST PAINT THEIR YO-YO AS THEY WISH. STICKERS CAN EMBELLISH OR COVER UP AS NEEDED.

Kitty's Favorite Treats

Yes, even your favorite feline deserves a treat for Christmas. Store these yummy tuna treats in made-for-kitty jars.

WHAT YOU NEED
(For the jars)

Canning jar, top, and ring
Kitty image (see page 186)
Ribbon, small pompons or jingle bells; tacky crafts glue

WHAT YOU DO

Color-copy or scan a kitty image from *page 186*. Draw around the jar top on the image and cut out. Glue to jar top. Fill the jar with Kitty Tuna Treats (*see recipe, below*). Place top on jar, then screw ring. Tie jingle bells or glue pompons on the end of ribbon; tie around jar. *Note: Be sure bells cannot be chewed from ribbon.*

Kitty Tuna Treats

1 cup wheat flour
⅓ cup wheat germ
3 tablespoons oatmeal
1 egg
1 tablespoon oil
6-ounce can tuna in oil, undrained

Combine all ingredients in a bowl and mix. Roll out to ¼-inch thickness. Cut into small fish shapes and place on an ungreased cookie sheet. Bake in a 350° oven for 20 minutes or until firm.
Not for human consumption—kitties only! Keep refrigerated for up to 2 weeks.

Evergreen Hat and Scarf

Knit this two-tone scarf and hat for someone dear to you. They'll love you all winter for it!

WHAT YOU NEED

Classic Elite GATSBY, 70% wool/15% viscose/15% nylon yarn (94 yards per bank):
For scarf; 2 banks of Green (2102) for MC and 1 bank of Turquoise (2172) for color A;
For bat; 1 bank of Green (2102) for MC and 1 bank of

Turquoise (2172) for color A.
Note: 2 banks green and 1 bank turquoise should be enough to make the set.
Size 10.5 (6.5mm) knitting needles or size needed to obtain gauge
Size 9 (5.5mm) knitting needles
Yarn needle

Skill Level: Easy

Size: Scarf measures approximately 46×6.5 inches, excluding fringe. Hat has a circumference of 24 inches.

Gauge: In Stockinette stitch with larger needles, 12 sts and 19 rows = 4"/10cm. Take time to check your gauge.

Notes: The hatband is worked in Stockinette stitch (St st) using two colors in each row. Carry color not in use loosely along WS of fabric. When changing colors, bring new strand from under present strand for a "twist" to prevent holes.

Special Abbreviation:
Ssk – slip next 2 sts singly and knitwise to right-hand needle, insert tip of left needle into fronts of these two stitches and k2tog.

Common Abbreviations:
k – knit
k2tog – knit together
MC – main color
p – purl
rep – repeat
RS – right side
st(s) – stitch(es)
WS – wrong side
Yo – yarn over

To wrap, use leftover yarn as the ribbon to tie around the package. Add tiny ornaments if desired.

Rows 16, 18, 20, 22, 24, 26: K2, p19, k2.

Row 17: K5, yo, ssk, k9, k2tog, yo, k5.

Row 19: K6, yo, ssk, k7, k2tog, yo, k6.

Row 21: K7, yo, ssk, k5, k2tog, yo, k7.

Row 23: K8, yo, ssk, k3, k2tog, yo, k8.

Row 25: K9, yo, ssk, k1, k2tog, yo, k9.

Row 27: K10, yo, (slip 1 stitch purlwise and with yarn on WS, k2tog, pass slipped stitch over k2tog – double decrease made), yo, k10 – 23 sts.

Row 28: K2, p9, cast on 1 st, p10, k2 – 24 sts.

Row 29: Knit.

Row 30: K2, p20, k2.

For scarf, rep Rows 1-30 for 6 times more. Bind off loosely and knitwise.

FINISHING

Place scarf onto a flat surface. Cover with a damp cloth and leave to dry.

continued on page 168

 WHAT YOU DO

SCARF

With larger needles and MC, cast on 24 sts.

PREPARATION

Row 1 (WS): K2, p20, k2.

Row 2: Knit.

Row 3: Rep Row 1.

BODY PATTERN

Row 1 (RS): K10, k2tog, yo, ssk, k10 – 23 sts.

Row 2: K2, p19, k2.

Row 3: K9, k2tog, yo, k1, yo, ssk, k9.

Row 4: K2, p8, k1, p1, k1, p8, k2.

Row 5: K8, k2tog, yo, p1, k1, p1, yo, ssk, k8.

Row 6: Rep Row 4.

Row 7: K7, k2tog, yo, (k1, p1) twice, k1, yo, ssk, k7.

Row 8: K2, p6, (k1, p1) 3 times, k1, p6, k2.

Row 9: K6, k2tog, yo, (p1, k1) 3 times, p1, yo, ssk, k6.

Row 10: Rep Row 8.

Row 11: K5, k2tog, yo, (k1, p1) 4 times, k1, yo, ssk, k5.

Row 12: K2, p4, (k1, p1) 5 times, k1, p4, k2.

Row 13: K4, k2tog, yo, (p1, k1) 5 times, p1, yo, ssk, k4.

Row 14: Rep Row 12.

Row 15: K4, yo, ssk, k11, k2tog, yo, k4.

FRINGE

Cut 5 strands of color A, each measuring 8 inches long. Hold strands in a bundle. Fold in half to form a loop. With the WS of the scarf facing and a size H crochet hook, take the loop through one stitch at end. Take ends through the loop and pull up to form a knot. Add fringe evenly across each end. Trim ends.

HAT

Beginning at the lower edge with MC and smaller needles, cast on 90 sts. (Purl 1 row, knit 1 row) twice for reverse St st . Change to larger needles.

Hatband

Row 1 (RS): (K3-MC, k3-A) across.

Row 2: (P3-A, p3-MC) across.

Rep Rows 1-2 until hatband measures approx 3 inches, ending with Row 1.

Change to smaller needles. Using MC, purl across.

Next Band: With MC and smaller needles, (purl 1 row, knit 1 row) twice. Knit 1 row.

Crown

With smaller needles and color A, purl 1 row, knit 1 row, purl 1 row.

Shaping

Row 1 (RS): K12; (k2tog, k13) across, ending k2tog, k1.

Row 2: P84.

Row 3: K11; (k2tog, k12) across, ending k2tog, k1.

Row 4: P78.

Row 5: K10; (k2tog, k11) across, ending k2tog, k1.

Row 6: P72.

Row 7: K9; (k2tog, k10) across, ending k2tog, k1.

Row 8: P66.

Row 9: K8; (k2tog, k9) across, ending k2tog, k1.

Row 10: P60.

Row 11: K7; (k2tog, k8) across, ending k2tog, k1.

Row 12: P54.

Row 13: K6; (k2tog, k7) across, ending k2tog, k1.

Row 14: P48.

Row 15: K5; (k2tog, k6) across, ending k2tog, k1.

Row 16: P42.

Row 17: K4; (k2tog, k5) across, ending k2tog, k1.

Row 18: P36.

Row 19: K3; (k2tog, k4) across, ending k2tog, k1.

Row 20: P30.

Row 21: K2; (k2tog, k3) across, ending k2tog, k1.

Row 22: P24.

Row 23: K1; (k2tog, k2) across, ending k2tog, k1.

Row 24: P18.

Row 25: (K2tog) across – 9 sts.

Leaving an 18" tail, cut yarn. Thread tail into yarn needle and back through rem 9 sts. Pull up to close opening. Use tail to join back seam.

Jeweled Wraps

Let these vintage
pins sparkle as
they decorate
your beautifully
wrapped package.

WHAT YOU NEED

Vintage jewelry pins
Wrapped packages without
  bows
Ribbon to coordinate with
  the jewelry

WHAT YOU DO

Wrap packages with solid
color papers. Decorate
with ribbon leaving the
ribbon flat. Pin the pins
to the ribbons.

Pretty Stationery Set

Vintage linens are cleverly folded to hold beautiful handmade stationery.

WHAT YOU NEED

Colored paper; rubber stamp

Ink pad; embossing powder

Heat gun; cardboard; scissors

Vintage linens; button

Needle and thread to match linen

WHAT YOU DO

For the stationery, cut paper to desired size. Stamp design on corner of paper and emboss with embossing powder. Use heat gun to activate powder. *To make holder,* cut the linen to a square shape and hem the edges or use a prehemmed square napkin. Cut cardboard slightly larger than the size of finished stationery. Lay the cardboard in the center of the square. Fold the sides and then the bottom over the cardboard. Tack with needle and thread. Fold top over and press. Sew button over top piece. Tuck stationery into the fabric envelope.

More Ideas
for gifts and wraps

 For the coffee lover on your Christmas list, fill an antique coffee cup with favorite coffee beans. Set the cup on the saucer. Cut a large square of cellophane and set the cup and saucer in the middle. Pull up all four corners of the cellophane and secure with a rubber band. Tie a bow over the rubber band. Add a tag that reads "Please come over for coffee during the holidays!"

Instead of wrapping your child's gift this year, wrap clues to find the gift somewhere in the house. Lead him or her all over the house with hints like, "Look under your math book" or "find your gym shoes and look inside them for the next clue." You'll be giving a treasure hunt as well as the gift.

 For the fast-food fellow on your list, purchase a gift certificate at his favorite place. Ask for an empty sandwich container at the same time. Put the certificates in the container, wrap with colorful tissue, and tie with curly ribbon.

 Copy and glue a favorite photo from a past Christmas event to the front of a 5×7-inch piece of colored cardstock. At the bottom write, "Wishing You The Joys of Today and Memories of Christmases Past" and frame the piece for a memorable gift.

 Fruit baskets make great gifts. This year add little goodies to the basket to make it extra special. Add favorite candies, colorful bottles of soda, playing cards, or unique kitchen utensils to personalize the gift.

 Use the fronts of old Christmas cards to cut into puzzle pieces. Put the pieces into a colorful envelope and take along for a "something to do" little gift for the kids while you drive to the mall to go Christmas shopping.

"For we have seen His star in the East, and we have come to worship Him."

—MATTHEW 2:2

watch the
season *glow*
with
**christmas
lighting**

A quick zig zag is all it takes to make this tree shine under the glow of a Christmas Eve candle.

Glowing Tree Candle

 WHAT YOU NEED

Tracing paper, pencil

Purchased three-wick candle

Ballpoint pen

Linoleum cutter (available at crafts and art stores)

Gold metallic acrylic paint

Soft cloth

 WHAT YOU DO

Trace the tree pattern, *below,* onto tracing paper. Lay the pattern over the candle and gently transfer the design onto the candle with a ballpoint pen. Repeat across the candle adding more stars in the open areas. Using the linoleum cutter, carefully carve the designs into the candle. Always carve away from yourself. Using your finger and gold paint, rub the paint into the carving. Wipe off excess paint with a soft cloth. *Never leave a burning candle unattended.*

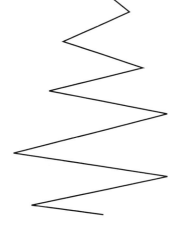

TREE SHAPE
PATTERN

**Make this
fun apple
candleholder
using two
apples in the
colors of
Christmas.**

*Christmas
Apple Holder*

 WHAT YOU NEED

*One red and one green apple
   approximately the same size
Apple corer/slicer
Rubber band
Gold doily
Small piece of gold trim
Straight pin
Taper candle*

 WHAT YOU DO

Set the apple corer/slicer
on top of each apple and
cut into pieces. Reassemble
the new apple holder by
alternating red and green
slices reforming them into
new apple shape. Secure
with a rubber band. Cut a
small circle from the doily
center. Cut a hole in the
center of the doily piece
and place over the top of
the apple. Put the gold
trim around the apple over
the rubber band and pin in
place. Set the apple on a
doily on a small dish.
Place the candle in the
apple holder. *Never leave a
burning candle unattended.*

Candy Candle

The glorious colors and shape of ribbon candy is all you need to make this clever candy arrangement.

MAKE IT TOGETHER

LET THE CHILDREN PICK OUT THE COLORS OF CANDY THAT MATCH OR COORDINATE WITH THE CANDLE. BE SURE TO HAVE ENOUGH EXTRA CANDY FOR MUNCHING.

WHAT YOU NEED

Purchased ribbon candy
Shallow glass dish
Pillar candle in color to
coordinate with candy colors

WHAT YOU DO

Set the candle in the middle of the dish.

We chose a glass dish with a decorative looped glass trim that repeats the loops of the candy. Arrange the candy around the candle. *Never leave a burning candle unattended.*

Beaded Holders

Watch the light shimmer through these glass beaded candleholders.

WHAT YOU NEED

Small purchased round candleholders

Glass beads to coordinate with holders

Strong crafts glue (such as E6000)

Votive candles

MAKE IT TONIGHT

WHEN YOU NEED A GIFT IDEA IN A HURRY, THIS IS THE PERFECT SOLUTION. YOU CAN MAKE TEN OR MORE HOLDERS IN AN EVENING AND HAVE THEM WRAPPED BY MORNING!

WHAT YOU DO

Wash and dry the candleholders. Choose beads in a size that just fits on the rim of the holder. Using beads that are in the same color family makes a pleasing arrangement. Using the crafts glue, glue the beads to the top of the holder. Allow to dry. Place candle in holder. *Never leave a burning candle unattended.*

Sanded Candles

Use desert-colored sand to secure votive candles in star-shape holders to depict the star that shone over the sand on that first Christmas.

WHAT YOU NEED

Colored sand (available at
craft stores)
Votive candles in desired colors
Glass star-shape holders
(available at craft stores)

WHAT YOU DO

Choose colors for the votives and the sand that coordinate. Carefully fill the glass containers with the colored sand. Place the votive in the sand. Add a card or book that depicts the first Christmas if desired. *Never leave a burning candle unattended.*

Sweet Spiced Candle

A pretty star shape
is even more pleasant
when it smells of
sweet oranges and
spicy cloves.

 WHAT YOU NEED

Star-shape gelatin molds

Awl

Custard cup

Small disposable pie tin

Whole cloves

Orange peel

White birthday candle

White candle wax

Small can for melting wax

Small saucepan

 WHAT YOU DO

Prepare mold by punching
hole in bottom of gelatin
mold with the awl. Place
custard cup in pie tin and
place mold on top. Put a
birthday candle upside
down in the hole. *(see below,
left)*. Put orange peel and
cloves into mold. Break up
wax and place in can and
then in saucepan of water.
(See *page 15* for wax
melting tips.) Heat wax
until just melted. Do not
overheat. *Never place wax in
microwave.* Pour a little wax
into the mold and let it set
for a few minutes. This will
seal around the birthday
candle and keep wax from
running though. Pour in
remaining wax. Let set
until hardened. Trim
bottom of excess birthday
candle. Invert candle to
remove from mold.
*Never leave a burning
candle unattended.*

Picture-Perfect Candles

Beautiful picture frames serve as stunning candleholders with just a clever touch of color.

WHAT YOU DO

Remove the back of the frame. Draw around it on a piece of cardboard and cut out. Cut a piece of fabric ¼ inch larger than the cardboard. Put the glass, then fabric, and then cardboard back in the frame. Secure in place. Turn over the frame and place candle on glass. *Never leave a burning candle unattended.*

WHAT YOU NEED

Picture frame in desired size
Cardboard
Scissors
Small piece of fabric to coordinate with candle
Desired color of candle

MAKE IT TONIGHT

HAVE THE FRAMES AND BITS OF FABRIC ON HAND AND THESE CLEVER HOLDERS CAN BE MADE IN A MATTER OF MINUTES. MAKE AN EXTRA SET AS GIFTS FOR SPECIAL FRIENDS.

Jewelry Ring

The flickering of
the candle makes
these vintage
jewels sparkle
with the season.

 WHAT YOU NEED
*9-inch foam wreath form
(such as Styrofoam)
Vintage jewelry
Hot-glue gun; glue sticks*

 WHAT YOU DO
Remove backs from
earrings and odd pieces
of jewelry if necessary.
Arrange on the wreath
form and glue in place
with hot glue. Work on
small areas at a time using
single earrings to fill in
small areas. Allow to dry.
*Never leave a burning
candle unattended.*

More Ideas
for Christmas lighting

 Use rope lighting to accent the most interesting outside areas of your house. The lights can be used to outline doors, windows, arches, porch railings, roof lines, or other unique features of your holiday home.

 Look for mismatched metal candleholders at flea markets and garage sales. Spray-paint all of them the same metallic copper color. Put various colors of brown-tone candles in the holders and arrange them on the mantle. Add pine cones and greens around the arrangement.

 Luminarias make a lovely statement as your guests arrive for the holidays. Place about 1 cup of uncooked rice in the bottom of various sized canning jars. Add red votive candles and a few red beads to the jars. Place the jars on the walkway or in the snow, and light the candles just before the guests arrive.

 Make a winter white centerpiece by filling a white dish or bowl with white beads. (Bags of beads are available at crafts stores.) Place three small white votive candles into the beads adjusting them to different heights.

 With a glass-paint marker, write the name of each guest on a clear votive candleholder. Place a votive candle in the holder and use this as the place card for each guest at your holiday party.

 For a quick lighting idea, arrange tiny Christmas ornaments in a small solid-colored bowl. Place a small candle in the center of the bowl of ornaments.

 Purchase a large colorful holiday candle. Use metallic gold and silver marking pens to write on the candle spelling out the words, "Joyous Noel" or "Joy to the World." Display the candle on a gold or silver tray.

Use these kitten
postcards with projects
on page 165

Hang up the stockings
Turn out the light
Make way for Santa
This is his night

Use these Christmas
postcards with projects
on pages 68–69.

A Merry Christmas to you

A MERRY CHRISTMAS

Use these Santa
postcards with projects
on pages 144–145

Use these Noah's Ark images to create the ornaments shown on page 151.

Index

Sources

EDIBLE GLITTER, DRAGÉES,
SNOWFLAKE-SHAPED COOKIE
CUTTERS, ORNAMENT-SHAPED
COOKIE CUTTERS, COLORED
SUGARS
Maid of Scandinavia by
Sweet Celebrations
(800)328-6722
www.sweetc.com
GLITTER
The Art Institute
www. artglitter.com
KNITTED HAT AND MITTENS
Classic Elite Yarns
(800)343-0308
E-mail: classicelite@aol.com
MICRO BEADS
Art Accents
www.artaccents.net
RIBBON
C.M. Offray & Sons
(800)344-5533
SPRAY PAINT
Design Master Paints
www.backgroundstobasics.com
QUILLING STRIPS
Lake City Crafts
(417)725-8444
www.quilling.com

If you like this book,
look for *Simply Christmas*,
available from Brave Ink
Press (www.braveink.com).

Acknowledgments

SPECIAL THANKS to all of these people who shared their unique talents to make this book possible: **Angie Hoogensen** for sharing her beautiful graphic design talent in designing the book. **Alice Wetzel** for rendering the sparkling watercolors featured throughout the book. **Pete Krumhardt** for sharing his enormous photographic talent and vision in the photographs featured in the book. **Andy Lyons** for giving of his creative photographic style and energy to the photos in the book. **Jennifer Petersen** for presenting food as art with her incredible cake and cookie decorating talent. And thanks to **B.J. Berti** who shared her creative ideas, opinions, and support in the making of this book.

A special thank you to my husband, Roger, and to my children, Michael and Elizabeth, who inspire me, support me, advise me, and continue to love me, no matter what the season.

This book is dedicated to my Mother who taught me the value of creativity, common sense, perseverance, and patience—and to see beauty in all things.

"God bless us every one!"

—A CHRISTMAS CAROL (1843)